AEROBICS
FOR
THE
SPIRIT

AEROBICS
FOR THE
Spirit

BOB
MORLEY

WORD PUBLISHING
Dallas · London · Sydney · Singapore

AEROBICS FOR THE SPIRIT: HOW TO BE HAPPY, HEALTHY, HOLY, AND HUMAN!

All Scripture quotations, unless otherwise noted, are from The Revised Standard Version of the Bible, copyrighted 1946, 1952, © 1971, 1973 by the Division of Christian Education of the National Council of the Churches of Christ in the U.S.A., and are used by permission.

The author gratefully acknowledges the following artists for permission to quote lyrics in part:

NATURE BOY © Golden World 1977.

THE PILGRIM: CHAPTER 33 (Kris Kristofferson) © 1970 Temi Combine Inc. All rights controlled by Combine Music Corp. and administered by EMI Blackwood Music Inc. All rights reserved. International copyright secured. Used by permission.

HE PLAYED REAL GOOD FOR FREE (Joni Mitchell) © 1967, 1974 Siquomb Publishing Corp. All rights reserved. Used by permission.

THAT'S WHAT FRIENDS ARE FOR (Carole Bayer Sager, Burt Bacharach) © 1982 WB Music Corp., Warner-Tamerlane Publishing Corp., New Hidden Valley Music & Carole Bayer Sager Music. Administered by WB Music Corp. & Warner-Tamerlane Publishing Corp. All rights reserved. Used by permission.

RED FLOWERS ARE RED © 1978 Story Song Ltd.

Library of Congress Cataloging-in-Publication Data:

Morley, Robert, 1943–
    Aerobics for the spirit : how to be happy, healthy, holy, and human! / Robert Morley.
        p. cm.
    1. Spiritual life—Methodist authors. 2. Spiritual exercises.
I. Title.
BV4501.2.M5855   1990
248.4—dc20   90-32702
                                                          CIP

ISBN 0-8499-0705-5
      0-8499-3224-6 (pbk.)

0 1 2 3 9 BKC 9 8 7 6 5 4 3 2 1

Printed in the United States of America

This book is dedicated to the people who rescued me in my floundering youth: Howard and Maime Kohler who listened to me as if what I had to say was important;

Claude Williams who always believed I was more talented than I was and was prepared to argue his case to the death;

C. B. Colaw whom God used in mysterious ways in my life, ways neither of us fully understand.

It's also dedicated to the Reverend Mark Trotter who has become for me a model for doing ministry. He embodies a standard of excellence for which I strive.

Contents

Foreword

When I first received the manuscript for *Aerobics for the Spirit* and was asked if I would be willing to write a foreword, I felt a bit awkward. It's one thing to have written a few books—another thing altogether to attempt to endorse someone else's work. I was, however, immediately drawn to Bob Morley when I found that he was a "piler" rather than a "filer." In this world of day-timers and organizational flow charts we need more creative spontaneity, vitality, and sheer love of life.

I know that I have occasionally been described as being "somewhere to the left of whoopee!" In Bob I found a kindred spirit. Reading between the lines, I sensed (as you will) a man who was indescribably passionate about everyday life.

He is audacious enough to write about the "practical" application of great spiritual truths in our daily lives. He is honest enough to be concerned with what we call the "ordinary" matters of life and bold enough to claim that they have eternal consequences. Because they *do!*

Listen . . .

Laugh . . .

Reflect . . .

Risk . . .

Grow . . .

We live in an age where the confusion is heightened and the pain has deepened. In the midst of this, Morley reminds us that Faith, Hope, Love, Joy, and Peace don't come in half sizes. He reminds us with fresh honesty that following Jesus Christ means more than just being able to sprinkle our sentences with a few pious phrases. In a spirited style, he challenges us all to close the nagging gap between our works and our lifestyle, between our doing and our being. He puts the *being* back in human. In a convincing manner this book confirms the foundational truths that many of us have long since taken for granted and invites us to new dimensions of living out this life-in-Christ—a life of greater integrity, a wounded yet infinitely deeper love, and an incorrigible hope in the fact that Easter is more than just a rumor.

He's spirited. He's a thoroughbred. This book is not intended to be a polite tap on the shoulder; it's more like a spirited jab in the ribs. His exercises will leave you winded at times—but you'll be stronger in the long run.

He encourages us to embrace life's contradictions, to leap into the paradoxes, and to celebrate the ironies that all of us face. He insists that there are some glorious incongruities in life, that we don't have to know all the answers in order to jump to the now—which I find absolutely refreshing. He doesn't offer easy answers—but uneasy questions. He gives us permission to sidestep some of the comfortable ooze of clichéd formulas and rediscover the delicious ambiguities of life as a "possibility" rather than an ordeal.

Morley's sense of humor is contagious. He has a unique gift for encouraging you to ponder life's deepest issues with a smile on your face.

On more than one page, Bob Morley does with words what Simon and Garfunkel did with music. He digs into the small print of reality to reflect in a new way on God's scandalous love for each one of us and His ever-new eternal story.

A good writer is a vivid storyteller. It's been affirmed that people grab onto and remember stories, parables, and anecdotes. He is an insightful storyteller who takes on the dangerous task of getting people to look at themselves.

These are the kinds of stories you'll find yourself telling again and again. This book is an invitation to the authentic life of the spirit. It speaks of a reality in Christ that transcends and exposes the shallowness of some of today's values.

Bob says, "If we don't change our direction, we are likely to end up where we are headed." Warning: the material contained between these covers could encourage you to alter the direction of your life. Don't just read this book. Absorb it into your lifestyle. Apply it. The result will be a tremendous, perhaps eternal, impact on the only life you can really change—your own.

This glorious "pile" of pages is fresh, original, and challenging. It is a veritable holy *yes* to that which is truly valuable.

Go for it!

Tim Hansel
La Verne, California
December 1989

Introduction

The Idea. It's been nearly a decade now since I met Dr. Bill Hetler. He and I were on the program of a YMCA convention in Bowling Green, Ohio. I caught his act and he caught mine; we were both genuinely impressed. Over coffee we began to compare journeys. Bill was the director of student services at the University of Wisconsin at Stevens Point and had just initiated a summer seminar on wellness. The idea was to pay some attention to our well-being as persons before we got sick and possibly avoid getting sick as often. As he outlined his program, he commented that he believed that there was a spiritual side to wellness as well as the usual physical and mental aspects. He said that he had lots of speakers on diet, exercise, stress management, and the like but was having some difficulty finding people to talk about spiritual wellness, especially without being too religious and too doctrinal about it. I took that as a challenge and during that same summer presented my first lecture on the subject. I have participated in that program about six times now in the past ten years and have finally decided to write something down. The outline for this book is based on those lectures at the Wellness Week in Stevens Point, Wisconsin.

I almost called this book "The Secrets of Life" but decided that that would sound a little ostentatious. I suspect, however,

that there are some secrets that will enrich your life buried somewhere in these pages of rambling and mumbling. If the secrets
are not actually here, at least this book may put you on their trail.

The Gift. In the words of Paul, "For I received from the Lord
what I also delivered to you" (1 Cor. 11:23). These stories and
insights are not mine to possess, they are gifts given to me that
must be shared. I have tried to present them in a form that will
help you to receive them with joy.

A Word about Style

This book is not so much a well-thought-out and organized
treatise as it is a gush of ideas. It is as much feeling as thought. I
hope it provides for you not so much memorable quotes, but a
new way of looking at yourself and your life. I offer these stories
about myself in the hope that you will be encouraged to claim
your story for the holy gift that it is.

This writing style is what some have called "stream of consciousness"; I just let one thing lead to another and sometimes the
whole thing comes back around to where it began. Have you ever
been involved in one of those long conversations in which you
seem to cover a hundred different subjects without being aware of
transitions? In retrospect it is hard to trace how you got from one
subject to the next: sometimes a key word or even an interruption
will be the stimulus that leads you off in a new and different
direction.

We are used to giving that liberty to other art forms: music,
graphic arts, dance, even drama, but not to writing. Since the
majority of our most detailed and technical information is con-
veyed by the written word we tend to assume and expect the
written word to be technical, pedantic, and highly organized. Yet
the written word—like every art form—has as one of its primary
purposes not just the transfer of information but the creation of a
mood, an aura. Art is like worship in that regard; in worship we
don't just say we praise God, we do it; we don't just say "God
loves us," we proclaim it and create a loving, sharing setting in
which the love of God can be experienced.

Thus I want this book to be more than a document that affects your head, more than a scholarly monologue; rather, I want this to be a conversation between us, one in which you are as much participant as I. Please let this writing affect you however you and it wants to—don't just read it, let it happen to you. If nothing happens to you, then use it for a doorstop.

Apology. All preachers keep files of potential sermon illustrations. These are often scribbled on napkins or on the backs of barf bags at 30,000 feet. They are collected at lectures or in elevator conversations. Sometimes other people who know of these collections will send a copy of a copy of a copy of something useful. Some of the material in this book has come from my collection. What that means, of course, is that some of the quotes may not be exactly correct and, more importantly, the person to whom credit should be given may have been lost or never known. I have done my best to provide sources; this is my apology to all of you unsung contributors to this book:

> I am my own research department and my
> research department is out to lunch a lot.

Confession. Did you know that all preachers preach to themselves? The points we punch the hardest in our sermons are the ones we most desperately need to hear ourselves. So lest you should assume that I am the walking, talking personification of all the principles I discuss in this book, please hear my confession. (I don't want you to be disappointed should we ever meet.)

I am susceptible from time to time to crummy attitudes and negative thoughts that put me on a downward spiral to depression and mess up my relationships, my self-esteem, and my joy in life. I have written what follows because they are the things that work for me if I constantly remind myself to practice them. D. T. Niles once described a Christian missionary as "one beggar telling another beggar where to find bread." I am not the guru here and you the novice; you probably know as much about this subject as I do. I share what I have learned along my journey in the hope that in the sharing with fellow pilgrims all our lives will be blessed and the spiritual health and beauty of us all will be made more excellent.

Acknowledgments

I applaud the patience of my congregation. Although the work on this book has taken time from my duties as a pastor and a preacher, they have been more than supportive.

Thanks also to my wife, Louise, who generously donated her typing skills and computer literacy to produce the final manuscript. Other helping hands generously donated along the way belong to Irene Dunny, who did the first batch of typing after hours in her spare time, and H. Hanson, who burned lots of midnight oil on my behalf.

A special thank you goes to Arralee Hays for doing all the hard work. It was she who convinced me to try for a book in the first place; she negotiated with the publisher and kept on encouraging me. She did much of the awful chore of translating my hand-written scratchings into typing *and* kept her good humor and sanity through it all. Thanks, Arralee.

1

From the Inside Out

*H*ave you ever noticed how many television commercials take place in the bathroom? There is some semi-dressed person applying a revolutionary new cosmetic in the hope of making him or her appear better than he or she actually is. Open any magazine and there they are again, plucking eyebrows, lengthening eyelashes, painting nails, covering zits, coloring gray hairs, hiding wrinkles, cinching in fat, and so on and so on. We owe it all to the mass media: this conviction universally and irrevocably held in our society that we can't possibly be lovable unless we are beautiful.

Perhaps we are so easily convinced because we already believed it in the first place. After all, how could anyone love us if we have double chins, bald spots, red eyes, and pimples? Being thus convinced we become a ready market for a never-ending flow of new products with secret formulas guaranteed to do the job; namely, to give us a more acceptable facade for the world to appreciate.

So the first order of business every morning is to go to work on that ragged exterior, to make it conform more to the image on the cover of a glamour magazine, a face anyone could love. The problem is that the person whose photo graces the cover of the magazine got up earlier than you did and has more expensive paint.

I have some good news and some bad news. The bad news is that the older you get the longer it takes to get made up. What a completely frustrating and depressing thought! No matter how much time, energy, expense, and dedication we put into this preservation/renovation project, we can never reverse the effects of time; we can only slow the process of deterioration. The lines will get deeper and more pronounced, the hair will gray, thin, and be less cooperative, the muscle tone will get more out of tune as we age. As one aging ballerina said to the other in the movie *The Turning Point*, "When I was young, my body used to complain. No one ever told me that someday it would out and out rebel!" What a depressing thought indeed to realize that all the high-tech paint and equipment known to modern science cannot make you look as good as you did when you were young and didn't need any fixing up at all. You used to wake up in the morning looking and feeling beautiful, but those days are irretrievably gone. So we spend an increasing number of hours in the bathroom trying to recover the magic of youth, that elusive glow of beauty. When the number of hours spent begins to edge toward twenty a day, it's hardly worth the effort anymore. That's the bad news.

The good news is that it doesn't matter! This whole exercise is based on a false premise. To be beautiful does not necessarily make one lovable! Beauty is a momentary attention-getting device; it causes others to step closer and see if there is anything about us worth a more prolonged investigation. If not, they go on their way. Beauty is the advertisement. What a shame if you spend so much energy on the advertisement that you don't have any left over to develop the product. Love is not the necessary response to physical attractiveness. External beauty has very little to do with love, real love, the kind that is an act of will and comes from a place within, which we call the "heart." Real beauty—the kind that does more than grab momentary attention but engages another's whole being for a lifetime—has little to do with external features. It is a beauty that comes from the inside out. Jesus had some strong words for those people in His day who made this silly mistake:

> Woe to you, scribes and Pharisees, hypocrites! for you
> cleanse the outside of the cup and of the plate, but inside
> they are full of extortion and rapacity. You blind Pharisee!

first cleanse the inside of the cup and of the plate, that the outside also may be clean.

Woe to you scribes and Pharisees, hypocrites! for you are like whitewashed tombs, which outwardly appear beautiful, but within they are full of dead men's bones and all uncleanness.

Matt. 23:25–27

The point is that everyone wants to be beautiful, and (if we are honest) we have to admit that external, physical beauty is of great importance to us. Some people, however, are born with a better chance at that than others. What I want to assert here is that there is a beauty that comes from the inside, a beauty that can be cultivated, which has a direct effect on how you are perceived by others. It's worth spending some time on if only to obtain the net result of being seen as outwardly more attractive.

So get out of the bathroom and into life! Spend less time and effort on damage control on the old exterior and more time and effort on sprucing up the inner self, the real you. Beauty that comes from deep inside is irresistible and not subject to the ravages of years, but rather is enhanced by them.

For example, I was on my way to church one Sunday when I saw two people walking side by side. Actually they were only beside each other for a brief moment, he was in fact passing her, but that moment was one of striking contrasts. He was what I hear referred to from time to time by the females of my acquaintance as a "hunk": young, tall, blond, muscular, athletic, gorgeous, looking like he had just stepped off the cover of *Gentlemen's Quarterly*. She was old, slow, overweight, and frumpy. She walked with a slight limp that made the uneven hem of her print dress jerk uncomfortably. She wore her drab gray hair in a granny bun and her drugstore spectacles slid to the tip of her button nose. What a study in contrasts they were!

You probably wouldn't believe me if I told you that my eyes were drawn more to her rather than toward him. There was a strange, indescribable beauty there. You see, he had no need or time to worry about inner beauty; he was a perfect physical specimen. Somehow the shriveled-up little spirit that rattled around in that man betrayed the fact that he was little more than a shell; if you scratched the surface of his personality you would find a vacuum. Not so with her. The glow of life that emanated from that little old funny body was irresistible. You could tell at a glance that that energetic, glowing spirit could not much longer tolerate being inhibited by that aging body it inhabited. Someday, not long from now, she would shed that vehicle like a snake sheds an outgrown skin and soar like a bird with newfound wings. The mixed metaphor is necessary to illustrate that the lovely spirit inhabiting that old body was a thing of beauty to behold. She had invested her time wisely.

I have in my files an article about an older woman in Louisville, Kentucky. I don't know where I originally saw it, but I have shared it in many settings. Whenever I read it, I think of that wonderful old lady I just told you about. I've often thought of these as words of wisdom from a healthy spirit:

> If I had my life to live over, I'd dare to make more mistakes next time. I'd relax; I would be sillier than I have been this trip. I would take fewer things seriously. I would take more chances. I would climb more mountains and swim more rivers. I would eat more ice cream and less beans. I would perhaps have more troubles, but I'd have fewer imaginary ones. You see, I'm one of those people who live sensibly and sanely hour after hour, day after day. Oh, I've had my moments, and if I had to do it over again, I'd have more of them. In fact, I'd try to have nothing else. Just moments, one after another, instead of living so many years ahead of each day. I've been one of those persons who never goes anywhere without a thermometer, a hot water bottle, a raincoat, and a parachute. If I had to do it again, I would travel lighter than I have. If I had my life to live over, I would start barefoot earlier in the spring and stay later in the fall. I would go to more dances. I would ride more merry-go-rounds. I would pick more daisies.

Moving is one of those adventures that helps us remember who we were and who we are and what is, after all, important. It happens when in the process of packing and unpacking that lifelong collection of our stuff, we uncover a treasure that we didn't remember having but couldn't possibly live without.

My own discovery was a photo album. What fun to be surprised by the ghosts of Christmas past with the turn of every

page, to stir up memories and emotions long since dormant and
believed gone. How quickly they came back to life, perhaps larger
than life, freed as they were from all the extraneous real-life issues
that were there when the shutter clicked. Now they are pure and
free to dance in my mind, touching hidden places.

There is a photo of my old dog Ezra. I can still laugh and weep
about times shared with him and his companion Lazarus, so
named because he had thick, black, matted hair and smelled like
he had been dead for three days. Also, when you called him, it
was like talking to a dead man. How proudly old Lazarus sat for
that photo, almost as if he knew that someday, long after he was
gone, that picture would be there to flood my heart with warm,
wonderful memories.

There's a picture of my mother before her false teeth. Her
teeth were crooked then with a funny little gap in the middle. She
used to say that's why she didn't like to smile for pictures. Her
new teeth are as straight as a picket fence, but she still doesn't like
to smile for pictures. Damn the orthodontist! Soon no one will
leave an interesting track in an apple or be able to do a decent
chipmunk impersonation.

Then there was my first girlfriend. She was thirteen and so was
I. I fell in love with her at an eighth grade graduation dance and
suffered the agony of that love all through my high school years. I
don't hesitate to use the word "love" to describe that early adolescent emotion. It was as real as any love since and perhaps more so,
because it was unencumbered by expectation and was offered in
pure childlike trust. My recollection of her after these years past
was of a beautiful little girl, or at least an intensely cute one. But
unless the picture had mysteriously deteriorated over those same
years, my recollection was incorrect. Staring back at me from the
photo album was the image of one who was sort of funny looking—round faced, frizzy haired, goofy grin. Why then had I remembered her as beautiful? The answer is easy—because I loved
her. I loved her spirit, her energy, her spontaneity, her sense of joy.
I loved what we shared: our first kiss on her grandmother's porch,
the time we cut down the church Christmas tree on her father's
farm and almost froze our feet. We rubbed each other's feet to
warm them up. That may be as close as one can come to true

intimacy. And the tree—it didn't look so big standing out there in
the middle of a forty-acre field. Once cut, it grew to a nearly un-
manageable size in the pickup truck. The top hung out the tail gate
while at least four feet of trunk was visible over the windshield.
There was no way it could fit through the church door. How we
laughed! We laughed when we cut the top third of it off to use in
the church. We laughed when we tried to hide the rest of it so no
one would discover our poor judgment. We laughed when people
told us later it was still too big. There was a special beauty in that
shared laughter which led us to share even more. We shared the
confusion and exhilaration of the first stirrings of religious faith
and of puberty. Our lives were woven together in a special way.
Our spirits made contact. Of course, I perceived her as beautiful;
she was beautiful—from the inside out.

I invite you to abandon the premise that making oneself beautiful makes one lovable as well. I submit that it is more accurately
stated exactly the opposite. Make yourself lovable and you will
be perceived as beautiful. In the next chapters I will offer some
exercises to get you started. None of them can be put into practice
in the bathroom, none of them will clear your complexion or hide
your gray hair, but, miracle of miracles, they might produce such a
glow about you that people don't even notice your external flaws
for the brilliance of your inner being. You can indeed become a
more beautiful person from the inside out.

Take heart! It may be too late for plastic surgery, but it is never
too late to experience the radical beautifying effects of a transformed spirit. William James said, "The greatest discovery in our
generation is that human beings, by changing the inner attitudes
of their minds, can change the outer aspects of their lives." And
the Apostle Paul said, "Do not be conformed to this world but be
transformed by the renewal of your mind" (Rom. 12:2).

The psychologists, philosophers, and theologians agree: you
can, by changing the way you think, change the way you are. A
local department store advertised recently a free "make-over." It
turned out that all they had to offer was a fresh coat of paint. A
make-over starts from the inside with who we are as thinking,
feeling creations of God; the outside is bound to be an expression
of that, for better or for worse. I invite you, no matter how

skeptical or cynical you are, no matter how far gone you think you are, to involve yourself in a spiritual "make-over." You are capable of transforming yourself to surprising degrees. As William James also said, "Man alone, of all creatures on earth, can change his own pattern. Man alone is the architect of his destiny." Invest yourself in things that beautify the spirit, and the consequent inner glow will obliterate surface flaws in ways that will astound both you and Max Factor.

> To the extent that you want to be thought of as beautiful try to find ways to make yourself lovable. Read on, there is help.

2

Defining the Indefinable

We human beings tend to see ourselves primarily as physical beings. We see each other coming and what do we see? A face that smiles, legs that walk, arms that reach out, a body to embrace. The physical is so immediate, so available. It's natural that we would think of ourselves as primarily physical, bodies that house minds and probably spirits. For that reason it naturally follows that we invest most of our time, energy, and money in the care and maintenance of our physical selves. All of that exercise equipment and those never-ending aerobic classes—not to mention health food, fad diets, and all-natural vitamin pills—are for the purpose of enhancing our physical well-being. Then there are hair colorings and cosmetics we use to make our physical selves look better than they really do, plus the hours spent looking into the bathroom mirror hoping against hope that the lines don't show and that the gray is covered. All of this we do with the full knowledge beforehand that ours is a lost cause. It's all downhill after about twenty-seven, and sooner than that for some people. We are going to get wrinkles and that's a fact. The only thing that might save us from the inevitability of gray hair is possibly going bald first. Our bones are going to get brittle, and our immune system is going to shut down. It's going to take longer and longer to recover from injuries, and (all that exercise not withstanding) our muscles will eventually turn to flab. It's a long downhill trek that leads inevitably to death, and all we can hope to do is to slow down the process of decline.

That's about all there is to say about our physical selves. So let's turn our attention to a more cheerful note and talk about our nonphysical selves.

The nonphysical is much more difficult to discuss because it is not as immediately available to us as the physical. The body gets most of the attention because it is so obvious, so readily available. It can be seen, touched, proven. It is predictable. If you feed it, it grows. If you stub it, it hurts. If you cut it, it bleeds. In other words, it fits easily into our understanding of what is real.

The nonphysical—that is, mind and spirit—requires other language and other images. They exist in a reality that isn't easily handled by the usual means. Of course we do take the nonphysical seriously, particularly the mind. We spend the first twenty years of our lives in schools training our minds. Then there are courses in speed reading and on improving our memories. There are endless adult education opportunities, seminars, training events all geared to help our minds grow and be more productive. All of this leads us to the good news that our minds don't start to decline at age twenty-seven. With some care and exercise our minds can continue to thrive for a lifetime. Then we die.

That leaves us with the spirit—that part of us that we spend very little or no time, energy, or money on, yet the spirit may be the only part of our being that continues to be when our bodies have shriveled up and dropped off, taking our minds down with them. If human beings could be divided into three parts (which of course they can't), those parts would be body, mind, and spirit, and spirit would be the most important and the least cared for, least understood, least discussed part of all.

My premise in this book is not only that each of us has a spirit but that we are primarily spirit. Whether we are religious or not, whether we have the appropriate language for it or not, whether we know it or not, we are not primarily a body housing a mind and spirit, but a spirit animating, for a time, *a* mind and *a* body. When the body and the mind wear out and are gone, the spirit that is you and me remains.

In order to deal with the reality of spirit we are going to have to develop a new language and risk abandoning our old ideas of what is real. Pilate may have asked Jesus the profoundest question ever when he sarcastically (or perhaps seriously) said to Him, "What is truth?" He probably didn't expect an answer. When you move into territory where there are no easy answers, no measurable quantities, no provable theorems, you are closer to truth than you think. At the very least you are searching in the right universe. If the history of our wars is always written by the winners, should you expect to find truth in them? Or do you trust a neutral observer—of which there are none? Is truth subjective—the way I see it is the way it is? Or is it pragmatic—if it works it is true? Is there such a thing as absolute truth? Is truth really beauty? (That's as good an answer as any.) We simply have to acknowledge that truth lies somewhere in the misty I-don't-know-for-sure area of life, along with its cousin, reality.

One of the axioms of life I have encountered in my own search for truth is that the more real a thing is the harder it is to describe. Things that can be measured, weighed, scientifically analyzed, bought, and sold are not reality, they are only props. You know you are talking about real things when you start using phrases like "it's sort of like this . . ." Real things can't be described; they can only be compared to something else. Truth cannot be known; it can only be pointed to and circumscribed. The language of reality is story.

When Jesus was asked about the kingdom of God, He told a story about a man who was walking across a field and found a treasure. Jesus was asked, "Who is my neighbor?" and He told a story about a man who got mugged and a foreigner who stopped to help. He was asked about forgiveness, and He told them a story about a father whose youngest son took his share of his inheritance and wasted it in a faraway land.

Just try to talk about love without telling a story. If love is the ultimate reality, how much does it weigh? What color is it? Where does it come from? Love is to life what spirit is to body. As love animates life, spirit animates body.

What I am saying is that if your definition of what is real is that which can be touched, defined, studied, and controlled, this discussion of spirit is going to be difficult for you. If, however, you

are willing to try a free-flowing definition of reality, then we can
move on. For our purposes here, try to stop thinking of yourself
primarily as a body and instead imagine yourself as a spirit animating a body. You are not a body housing a mind and spirit, but a
spirit giving life to a body and a mind. The question is not "Do
you have a spirit?" but rather "Are you a spirit?" Spirit, not body,
represents the reality of you.

About Categories

You are now several pages into this book and perhaps trying to
decide if it is religious or not. We love to put things in nice, neat
categories, don't we? It makes life so manageable; never mind that
life become manageable is not life at all. Still, some of you bought
this book because you thought it was going to be a religious book,
and now you aren't so sure. Maybe it is more a philosophy book or
a psychology book. Perhaps it's a comedy or an autobiography.
Under which heading should it be filed? Don't! Resisting the
temptation to systematize, organize, and categorize things may be
your first step toward a healthier spirit.

I have taken upon myself the task in this chapter of defining
the indefinable. I want to offer you some sense of what I am
talking about when I talk about spirit. Due to the elusive nature
of the subject, that definition has to come in the form of allusion
and even illusion. It comes in stories that evoke feelings rather
than conveying information. If you try to categorize it, you may
miss it. Trust me, just let it pile up.

One of the biggest frustrations of my life is my filing system,
if I dare even call it that. The word *system* always sticks in my
throat. But information does come in, sometimes in the mail, or I
find usable information in books and magazines, information that
I want to file away so that it will be easily retrievable when I need
it. The problem is that most of the things that interest me are
things that don't lend themselves to obvious categories, so it
collects in piles on my desk, odds and ends, thises and thats. One
pile becomes several, and then everything loses its distinctiveness
and merges into one giant pile again. It's a metamorphosis to
behold with wonder.

From time to time I get down on myself and insist that a

rational adult ought to be able to develop a simple filing system. The moment usually comes when part of the stack tips over and spreads itself across the floor. It's time to take decisive action, so I file all that stuff. My desk is clean. I am amazed at how big and black its top is—it's been so long since I've seen it in its entirety. I invite my secretary and other work associates in to witness the spectacle of the empty desk. They are in awe. Of course I know that when I go to retrieve that filed information I will never be able to find it because I won't remember what category I filed it under. I'll try to retrace my steps mentally, but I come to a different place every time. So I invariably revert to the old system—the pile. Those of us who use the pile system rather than the file system can't seem to avoid being defensive about it. We know that those clean desk types out there see our system as no system at all. But in terms of its efficiency in retrieving information, the pile system has always worked better than the file system for me.

I met a San Francisco artist once who invited me to his studio, to the place where he actually did his work. He let me know that not everyone was welcome there, just kindred spirits. It was an inner sanctum. I was honored. He was primarily an abstract artist, which I suppose accounted for our sense of spiritual connectedness.

Since an abstract artist never knows where a stroke will end, he must have a large easel to accommodate huge canvases. His was the size of a barn door. His brushes were standing in some Folger's coffee cans, and there were two folding tables piled high with tubes of paint, all of them without caps and squeezed from the middle. There must have been a hundred tubes, maybe more, arranged with no visible system at all, just piles. He insisted that he could reach into those two piles and pull out exactly the color he wanted, and if anyone came in and moved one of his tubes, he would know it. Instantly I understood the real reason for our sense of being kindred spirits: he was a piler too!

This book will be more helpful to you if you are a piler. If you are a piler you realize that religion cannot tolerate existing within its own separate category. Religion is only relevant when piled in with everything else that makes up the marvelous hodgepodge that is life. Indeed, if anything has spoiled and emasculated religion in our time, it is that it has been neatly filed into a separate category, away from our social life, away from our family relations, away from our business dealings, our politics, and our moral and ethical decision making. Religion has been successfully domesticated. Where once it was the salt that added spice to life, the leaven that made the lump of life grow and rise; where once religion informed, shaped, and did battle with all the other categories of life, now it sits passively by, off to the side of life, hardly noticed or acknowledged. Is it any wonder that most of society has abandoned it altogether? It is now a harmless curiosity, a toothless relic of our past. Churches are the museums in which it is housed. By allowing itself to be removed from the pile, religion has lost not only its relevance but its reason to be.

For example, music has always been a part of my life, and I have performed with guitar and voice since childhood. People naturally assume that since I am a Christian I necessarily perform so-called Christian music. But what makes a song "Christian," I ask? If Jesus is mentioned in the lyric, is that enough? What about all those songs that deal with the complexities of life, about relationships, higher values, and the joy of life? Are they by definition not religious? Is "Greensleeves" a secular song and "What Child Is This?" a sacred one? If it's played as an instrumental which is it? And what about music that by its glorious character transports listeners beyond themselves and into the presence of the divine, even if for just a moment? Was Beethoven's Ninth Symphony religious before its theme was used as a hymn tune? Why must we categorize everything as sacred and secular? All creativity is divine. All beauty is sacred. Anything that reaches down and touches something inside us and calls us to better and higher planes is of God.

Spirit cannot be confined, categorized, or even defined; it just is. If we will try to let our rational minds be a little more free flowing and unleash the images that speak of that other intangible reality, perhaps we will not only be able to define the indefinable but also know the unknowable. God is not known by rational means. God cannot be discovered. God is only known by revelation. And God is spirit!

To be created in the image of God means that human beings are essentially religious beings. To ignore that essential aspect in the doing of life is to relegate the whole experience of living to a never-never land of incompleteness and unfulfillment. The religious person (that's all of us) must make religion a part of the pile that is life and then jump into the middle of it just for the joy of it.

A Word about Words

These are bold assertions: that all people are religious and that religion permeates and conditions all of life. If these assertions are correct, then the most insidious categorizations of all would be those called sacred and secular. That which is sacred cannot exist apart from the rest of life. Therefore it persists in climbing out of its filing slot and getting into all the others. This truth is evidenced by the observable fact that religious words are continually crossing over into secular usage. They refuse to stay in their separate file folders. They move back into the pile, and we welcome them because we suspect that they are the glue that holds it all together and fills in the mysterious blanks in our existence.

A few of those words that have crossed over are *commitment, grace, faith,* and even *born-again.* "Born-again" is a distinctly religious phrase adopted by a particular type of religious person, the so-called Christian evangelical. All religious people choose metaphors and word pictures to describe the indescribable, coming-alive experience of coming into contact with God's spirit. Some Christians have seized upon this phrase as the ultimate. "Born-again," that says it better than any other. It is categorically a religious phrase, the property of the religious community, used to describe religious experience, borrowed right out of the Gospel of John. It is also, however, a phrase used to make categories even narrower. Some are not satisfied with being just Christian, so they use the term to identify themselves as a particular type of Christian, thus putting themselves into an even smaller and more exclusive file.

What a surprise it was when "born-again" cropped up in the lyrics of a popular song describing the experience of newfound romantic love. The singer crooned "with you I'm born again." Then other people began to use the phrase to describe a variety of renewing, awakening experiences not at all religious: a new job, a face-lift, a geographical move, quitting drinking or smoking, beginning an exercise program. They say, "It's as if I were born-again!"

If "born-again" can cross over into the categories of secular life, then it is certain that other religious words could follow. For example, "commitment" is a word that belongs to religion. We Christians talk about commitment to Christ as the key tenet of our faith. The Bible calls our relationship with God a covenant. In order to establish that covenant with God, or with another person, commitment is a primary requisite.

When I counsel persons about marriage, I tell them that marriage is a covenant made in the presence of God and that commitment is the primary issue. It's not the question answered "I do" that is most important, the important question is the one answered "I will." The question isn't "Do you love one another?" but "Will you love one another no matter what happens or what surprises the future holds, for richer or for poorer, in sickness and in health, even if you grow fat and ugly and the passion all dies, for the rest of your lives whether you feel like it or not?" That's an act of commitment!

Lately, I keep seeing the word *commitment* printed full length across my television with the smooth flowing voice of a professional announcer telling me that it describes how a bank does business or how a car manufacturer feels about my safety. Commitment has moved from the realm of religion to that of life, making both more relevant. Religion and life are thus seen as being in covenant relationship with commitment as its primary requisite.

One of the loveliest words of all time is *grace*. Grace has been described by Frederick Buechner in his book *Wishful Thinking* as one of the least shopworn of all religious words:

> Mysteriously, even derivatives like 'gracious' and 'graceful' still have some of the bloom left.
> Grace is something you can never get but only be given. There's no way to earn it or deserve it or bring it about any more than you can deserve the taste of raspberries and cream or earn good looks or bring about your own birth.

A good sleep is grace and so are good dreams. Most tears are grace. The smell of rain is grace. Somebody loving you is grace. Loving somebody is grace. . . .

The grace of God means something like: Here is your life. You might never have been, but you are because the party wouldn't have been complete without you. Here is the world. Beautiful and terrible things will happen. Don't be afraid. I am with you. Nothing can ever separate us. It's for you I created the Universe. I love you.

With grace thus defined, is it any wonder that the most popular religious song of our century is "Amazing Grace"? Yet we were all a bit surprised when it became a Top 40 hit a few years ago and when it still crops up from time to time in bluegrass idioms or in elevators or even on bagpipes. "Grace" is much too marvelous a word to be shunted off to the irrelevant fringe of life; it insists on its rightful place on the main stage.

M. Scott Peck in his great book *The Road Less Traveled* titled the whole closing section of his book "Grace." Peck is a psychologist, not a theologian, yet he asserts that grace is everywhere operative in common life and that its most salient feature is that it is, in fact, amazing. It is amazing, observes Peck, that people are as healthy as they are and that when they get sick they usually get well again. It is amazing that there are relatively few accidents with so many cars zipping around on our multilane freeways. All of this is grace!

"Grace" is a word that has crossed over quite simply because it can never be confined or controlled. Grace is by definition free and can never be considered as the exclusive prerogative of that part of life we call religious. It belongs to the masses and the ages; it is life's juice.

Faith is the most religious word of all. It is the other word for religion; indeed they are used interchangeably or in tandem, as in "religious faith." For the religious, faith is the alpha and the omega; it is the goal and the method by which the goal is achieved. Buechner says in *Wishful Thinking*, "Faith is better understood as a verb than a noun, as a process than as a possession. It is on-again-off-again rather than once-and-for-all. Faith is not being sure where you're going but going anyway."

"Faith," although it is the most religious of all words, has also crossed over. As a greeting, people casually say to one another, "Have faith." There seems to be an instinctive understanding of the meaning of the word, and since that understanding is innate and universal, there is no need to define it. If pressed for a definition, the word *belief* would come up, but everyone knows they don't mean the same thing. Faith is what holds together when beliefs fall apart.

Harry Emerson Fosdick wrote in *The Meaning of Faith*: "Faith is holding reasonable convictions in realms beyond the reach of final demonstration, and, as well, it is thrusting out one's life upon those convictions as though they were surely true. Faith is vision plus valor."

Anyone who gets on an airplane has faith. Is it really logical or sensible to believe that those tons of sheet metal and rivets can fly? Yet we regularly pack our suitcases and stake our lives on that conviction. We walk onto that machine without the slightest question or fear. Our hearts don't flutter; our palms don't sweat. We simply fasten our seat belts and grab a magazine. But our faith goes even deeper than that. How many of us have ever been inclined to look into the cockpit to be sure a pilot was up there? (And if he is, how can you be sure he has really had flying lessons?) How do you know there is fuel in the tanks? We don't know these things—we take it, as they say, by faith.

The whole world operates on faith, otherwise no one would set foot outside the house in the morning. "Faith," Fosdick says, is that by which "we discover ourselves, the outer world's existence and its unity . . . faith is always the Great Discoverer."

Then there is spirit! *Spirit* is one of those wonderful words that moves easily across the boundary between what is religious and what is secular. Spirit is, of course, an important word in the religious person's lexicon; it is after all one of the ways in which we understand and address God. But spirit is just as much at home in the world of everyday life and events. There is school spirit, team spirit, the spirit of friendship, one's being spirited away, the Spirit of St. Louis, and, of course, alcoholic spirits. It is such a comfortable word for people in general that I'm not going to make an attempt to define it. To define it is probably to ruin it because the very nature of spirit is mystery.

Spirit is always elusive, always nebulous, always moving and changing. If we could define it, our definition would be obsolete in the very next instant. To define is to control, to categorize is to confine, and the spirit will have none of that.

We Christians understand God as Trinity—Father, Son, and Spirit. We have given names to the first two. Father is Yahweh, Elohim, etc. Son is Jesus. But Spirit is only Spirit. To name a thing is to define it, so Spirit remains nameless in the Trinity. Father and Son are relational terms, but not Spirit. You can't name the un-nameable or define the indefinable or assign a function to ultimate reality. So we won't try. We will just let it be. When Spirit spoke to Moses out of a burning bush, Moses asked if he could know the name of the one who spoke. "I Am" was the answer. Spirit is pure being.

All of this is wonderfully illustrated in a conversation Jesus had with Nicodemus. You must understand that Nicodemus was both a teacher and a Pharisee. Pharisees were religious legalists. They liked everything spelled out in concrete terms. They reduced religion to a list of rules, laws of conduct, so that at any moment in life you could get an accurate reading of your religious well-being. It was the prototype for the checklist, pulse-taking religion that is still around today. Nicodemus was also a teacher. In order to teach, teachers have to break things down into their component parts. Information comes in small bits and in logical succession. That's how students learn. There is a step one, step two, and step three about everything. So you teach them how to diagram a sentence, to memorize the multiplication tables, and to carry the one to the ten's place. That was the mind-set out of which Nicodemus asked Jesus to talk about ultimate reality.

Jesus told Nicodemus that you can't talk about spirit in absolute terms. "That which is born of the flesh is flesh, and that which is born of the Spirit is spirit" (John 3:6). Then he painted a word picture for him and said, "It's kind of like this. The wind blows wherever it wants to and you don't know where it comes from or where it is going but you feel the power of it." Wouldn't you know it, the Hebrew word for spirit is the same as the word for wind. When God breathed into Adam the breath of life in the Genesis story, what was breathed was spirit/wind. In the church we talk about the movement of the spirit. That's a very precise phrase because if spirit is like wind, then you are only aware of it when it moves. Yet where and when and why it moves remains a glorious mystery.

Poor old Nicodemus wasn't into mystery. He couldn't get his rational mind around this concept any more than he could the metaphor of being born again. His way of thinking was so structured as to be unable even to see that a metaphor was intended. He scratched his head, shrugged his shoulders, and said, "I think I'm too big for that." If we are going to think about spirit at all, we need to change the way we think, we must learn to embrace mystery, unknowability, and surprise.

The charismatic movement's renewed emphasis on speaking in tongues illustrates this phenomenon better than any event in recent years. The evidence for its being an authentic movement of the Spirit was that it came as a surprise. No one planned it or prompted it, but there it was. It didn't happen where it was supposed to happen. Pentecostal churches had always emphasized speaking in tongues in their worship, so you would naturally expect it to happen there. But it started happening among the Catholics and Episcopalians who had no frame of reference for it, and it raised a furor. It was very disconcerting to have someone jump up and spout off during a dignified liturgical worship service. Many of these people found themselves ostracized, so they went off and formed their own organizations around the phenomenon that bound them together. They called them charismatic churches. Now the spirit had a place to move where no one would be upset. But you can't institutionalize the movement of the Spirit, you can't capture the wind, and you can't stage a happening. The churches remain; the Spirit has moved on.

The movement of the spirit is in no way exclusively a religious experience. Spirit is part of the language and experience of the secular world. Perhaps you remember a concert where the music had a particular power and buoyancy about it and you found yourself caught up and swept away. Remember the first time you heard Beethoven's Ninth Symphony? Did the spirit blow through your being in a peculiar and unique way? One of the prerogatives of spirit is to inspire or breathe itself into people in an enlivening way. We say the writers of the Bible were inspired. Perhaps the same spirit that blew through Matthew, Mark, Luke, and John also blew through Shakespeare, and Hemingway, and, on a particularly good day, Beethoven. Maybe it happened to you, perhaps in a moment of great joy or deep sorrow, in the embrace of a loved one, in surprising times of personal creativity and playfulness—you felt the wind of the spirit blow through you.

I was lucky enough to hear Simon and Garfunkel on the concert tour in which they introduced "Bridge over Troubled Waters." There were eighteen hundred people in the Long Beach Arena that night. When the song was over, there was not a sound. The deafening silence hung in the air for several minutes—no applause, no sound. Then the concert went on. What could make eighteen hundred people—religious, nonreligious, young, old, introspective, and boisterous—all agree to be perfectly silent when our training and culture would have us applauding? That moment couldn't have been orchestrated in a million years except for the power of the spirit that blew into the place, and for a moment in time we were as one. Jesus said, "The wind blows where it wills, and you hear the sound of it, but you do not know whence it comes or whither it goes" (John 3:8). Do you ever feel the power?

That spirit and your spirit are part of the same fabric. In the movie *Little Big Man*, Chief Dan George explains to Dustin Hoffman the difference between the white man and the Indian. The white man, he says, believes that everything is dead, and so he conducts himself accordingly. The Indian believes that everything is alive, not just men and animals, but the rocks, the trees, the river. They all have life. They all share the spirit. For the Indian, all of life was a giant tapestry. If any part of that life was diminished, it diminished everyone. That's why they prayed before they killed a buffalo. That's why they used every scrap of its carcass. They believed that what they killed became a part of them.

That great spirit that blows through all creation also blows through you and gives you life and defines you. You are spirit!

Conclusion

If human beings could be divided into three parts, they would be spirit, mind, and body. But, of course, we can't be easily compartmentalized. Physicians have known this since wizards first made magic potions and witch doctors threw bones and beads across the floors of their huts. The mind has a profound effect on the healing of the body. You often hear doctors talk about the will to live. Positive, hopeful people tend to recover from illnesses easier and quicker. Happy people don't get sick as often.

As mental attitude affects the physical positively or negatively, so the reverse is true. What is sometimes diagnosed as a mental/emotional ailment may in fact be symptomatic of a physical problem. Depression and schizophrenia can be brought on by a chemical imbalance in the body. So the doctor who treats the body may focus his treatment on the mind and a doctor who treats the mind may be looking at physically induced symptoms.

Suppose the root of an ailment doesn't lie within the realm of body or mind. Suppose the cause is in that nebulous, mysterious world we call spirit, that part of our being on which we spend no time, money, or energy because we don't understand it. Indeed we can't even find it. Can the spirit be treated?

In order to enhance the health and beauty of our whole being we must have spiritual—as well as physical and mental—well-being. If indeed it is possible to exercise the body and mind to make them healthier, more productive, and more resistant to disease and decline, is it not also possible to exercise the spirit for the same reason? a sort of aerobic program for the spirit?

That is our goal for this book, to suggest ways of exercising the spirit with a final goal of making it healthier. That healthy spirit then animating the body and mind will make for a more beautiful person from the inside out. I can't tell you why or how these things seem to work, they just do. Maybe it's all a placebo. But who cares why it works as long as it works? I am so sure of the success of this health and beauty treatment that it comes with a guarantee. Look for it at the end.

In *The Meaning of Faith* Fosdick tells this story: "John Quincy

Adams at the age of eighty met a friend upon a Boston street. 'Good morning,' said the friend, 'and how is John Quincy Adams today?' 'Thank you,' was the ex-president's reply, 'John Quincy Adams himself is well, quite well, I thank you. But the house in which he lives at present is becoming dilapidated. It is tottering upon its foundations. Time and the seasons have nearly destroyed it. Its roof is pretty well worn out. Its walls are much shattered and it trembles with every wind. The old tenement is becoming almost uninhabitable and I think John Quincy Adams will have to move out of it soon. But he himself is quite well, quite well.'"

Remember, the real you is spirit, giving life to a body and a mind.

Repeat this creed: I am spirit. I have a body and a mind, but I am spirit! Then work to get rid of all of the compartments of your life, particularly that distinction between what is secular and what is sacred. Let your life be rather a marvelous montage of the tangible real and the intangible and indescribable real and let it all be a glorious pile energized by spirit.

3

Come Out and Play

*T*hose are magic words. They can't help but sweep us back across the years to a time when life was full of short agendas, long summer days, and good friends who would hurry through supper just so they could ride their bikes over to your house and yell through the screen door, "Can you come out and play?" At what age do we stop asking that question—and why? Why should we cease asking one another the most magical question of all? That question was the gateway to tree houses, or secret hiding places, or the wild West, or the jungles of darkest Africa, or the invasion of Normandy; all within the range of your mother's voice saying, "Come in now, it's getting dark." But the question does stop being asked, that's why it always reminds us of our childhood, because no one asks it when you are an adult.

Philosophers have suggested for centuries that life ought to be seen as play. The gods of the Greeks used mortals as pawns in some gigantic board game of their own devising for their own enjoyment. Perhaps life should be seen as a marvelously intricate practical joke that's being played on you. Maybe board games like Monopoly imitate life so well because life is, after all, a game. If you land on the wrong square, you go directly to jail, do not pass go, do not collect $200. But with a little luck you can own a hotel on Park Place *and* a railroad monopoly. Win or lose, you can laugh. Sidney Harris observed, "God could not be solemn, or he would not have blessed man with the incalculable gift of laughter." If life is a game, then the proper response to it is laughter, to respond with joy to the invitation to come out and play. Sometimes you're "it" and sometimes you're "home free," but always you laugh and then sleep the sleep of the blessed.

One way to tell sane people from crazy people is to note what they laugh at. Crazy people laugh at inappropriate times. Sane people laugh at themselves and the circumstances in which they find themselves, even tragic ones. That's why the contemporary crop of comedians is so helpful. People like George Carlin and Richard Pryor find their humor in the everyday events of their lives. Bill Cosby built the most popular show on television on the same kind of day-by-day experiences.

Richard Pryor even found humor in his near-death experience. What could possibly be funny about this tragic picture: a poor, lonely rich man, sitting in his mansion, mixing up drugs to placate his addiction and soften his sense of loneliness? The whole thing blew up in his face, literally, and he suffered third-degree burns over much of his body and nearly lost his life. How can that be funny? Later, on stage, he quipped, "When you're running down the street on fire, people will get out of your way."

In his book *Man's Search for Meaning*, Viktor Frankl tells of the time he was taken to a Nazi concentration camp. The newcomers were being instructed on what to expect from life in the camp. "As long as you are strong and can work," the lecturer said, "you will do fine, but if you are weak and sickly, you won't survive." Then he pointed at Frankl and said, "Like you." Frankl says that he laughed. At that moment, he discovered one of life's basic principles: an abnormal reaction to an abnormal situation is normal. Laughing to keep from crying is normal and healthy. We might also note that Viktor Frankl lived to tell the story with a twinkle in his eye.

The great preacher of another century, Henry Ward Beecher, said, "A person without a sense of humor is like a wagon without spring—jolted by every pebble in the road." I have never spent any time in a prison camp, but I've had some off days. Sometimes you know from the way the day starts that it's going to go from bad to worse. You stub your toe on a table leg that has been in that exact spot for years. You look in the mirror and your hair has a wing no amount of Dippity Do will smash down. I observed long ago that as your hair goes, so goes your day. If you were smart, you would crawl back into bed and pull the blankets up over your head. That, we all know, is the safest place in the world. The creatures that live under the bed and in the hall closet can't get you if the covers are pulled up, and neither can anything else. As a boy, I was taught to go to the cellar during a tornado and to get under my desk in case of a nuclear attack, but something inside me always knew that the only safe place from storms and other outrageous blasts was in my own bed with the covers pulled up.

But for some reason, on those everything-is-going-to-go-wrong days, we don't rush to that safe harbor and wait till the storm blows over. We stay up and at it. We do this to prove to ourselves that our instincts and our hair were correct in their predictions. There is some satisfaction to be gained from having your predictions validated, even if you are predicting a miserable time for yourself.

Sometimes I find "party" questions hard to answer. Questions like: What is your favorite thing to do? What was your most embarrassing moment? What do you want to be when you grow up? But I have an immediate answer for one of these questions. It leaps to mind without hesitation whenever it's asked. What was the worst day of your life? Let me offer here a brief synopsis of my answer.

The year was 1976. I remember that clearly because I was going to Philadelphia and glad to be going to the nation's birthplace on the bicentennial year. In those days, I was traveling the country in a van, doing musical programs for churches, schools, and anyone else who would invite me. It was a travel day that began in Cleveland. (There have been so many jokes about Cleveland that I will avoid the urge to further insult that city; suffice it to say that I agree with whoever it was who first observed that "dying in Cleveland is redundant.") I woke up early, stubbed my toe, and my hair was out of control. Neither my schedule nor the checkout time of the motel would allow me to jump back in bed and pull the covers up.

It was raining that day like it rains in Ohio. In other places the rain seems to wash things off and bring a certain cleansing and renewal. In Ohio it rains dirt. Add to the grayness of the dismal day the fact that I had already been on the road for nearly two months, and the idea of yet another day of driving was not a very welcome or invigorating thought for me or for my canine traveling companion, Gypsy. But I checked out of the motel and hit the road, all the time feeling that this was going to be a bummer of a day.

There was the usual array of rude and aggressive drivers, traffic tie-ups on the Pennsylvania Turnpike, and awful roadside restaurants. The only bright and hopeful moment came when one of those high-powered cars passed me at nearly double my speed. Those are the people you wish would get a ticket, but they never do. A few miles up the road, I saw that he had been pulled over by the state patrol. He passed me again later and, just like in a fairy tale, I passed him again doing business with another state patrolman. I think of that story whenever I start to doubt if there is any justice left in the world. How ironic that my paradigm of justice would come out of Pennsylvania.

Finally, Philadelphia loomed on the horizon, just about sunset. Not having a motel reservation, I decided to stop at the first Holiday Inn or Ramada Inn I saw. I didn't see any. By now it was dark, still raining, and I was almost through Philadelphia. I took the next exit. There was a sign flashing the word *Motel*. It was a seedy looking place, but I was tired, and it would do. The room was average: cigarette burns on the carpet and the top of the television, the smell of mingled stale smoke and heavy disinfectant wafting in the air. I dumped my suitcase, opened all the windows, and headed for the motel restaurant. They didn't have a restaurant, but I was given directions to a nearby bowling alley. I sat alone in the bowling alley coffee shop for several minutes until an unpleasant employee informed me that they didn't serve food, not even coffee. Never having heard of a coffee shop that didn't serve coffee, I asked if they knew of one that did and was given directions to yet another unpleasant establishment. Technically, they didn't serve food either, but they did bring me something to eat.

As I sat there watching the mystery meat float around on my plate while the rain pounded the slums of Philadelphia, I thought to myself, this has got to be the worst day of my life. But the gods of misadventure weren't through with me yet.

Back at the motel I had just double locked the door and settled in for the night when the phone rang. It was the motel manager, "Is that your blue van in the parking lot? It's been broken into." Sure enough, the side window was smashed, my guitar and part of my sound system were gone, and the rain was pouring in the open window, soaking the seats and carpets. I moved the van under the canopy and went to call the police. Their response can best be described as uncaring, unsupportive, and unpleasant. Their interest lay not so much in taking a report as scolding me for being dumb enough to park my van in that neighborhood. I tried to impress upon them the importance of the guitar. Guitars are not replaceable. For one thing they get better with age. The more you play your guitar, the more it seems to adapt itself to your touch. I had a twelve-year relationship with that Martin D-35, and it wasn't as if I could take the insurance money and go out and buy another one. The guitar is among the most intimate of instruments. You hold it to your body and stroke it with your hands; its voice and yours become one, your overtones resonate together. It wasn't just another guitar, it was part of me, like a very special friend.

The officers were unimpressed with my poetic plea. They actually laughed when I offered them the guitar serial number. They had no intention of looking for it. "Buy another one," was their advice, and they left.

I spent the rest of the night shivering in the van to protect it from further "ripoffs" and looking forward to the next day when my agenda would include finding a substitute guitar for my program that evening and getting my window fixed. The glass man charged me three times the usual fee because he noticed my out-of-state plates.

That's the story of the worst day of my life. The recollection remains vivid after all these years. It probably compares well with some of your days. Even though I mourn the loss of that guitar to this day and have a certain loathing for Philadelphia and especially Philadelphia cops, I still see some humor in it. The recollection of the worst day of my life does not fill me with rage. I have found a little mirth in it. I take that as a sign of a healthy spirit and I rejoice. Of course, it took a while for me to find the humor in it. Most of the funny things we tell our friends about ourselves were not funny at the time. I drove out of Philadelphia with my foot on the floor and my mind racing with plans to put bars on the windows and electrify the whole cab so that the next person who tried to invade the sanctity of my Chevy van and kidnap my friend with whom I sang would end up as little more than a grease spot on the parking lot. From my motel room I would hear the sound of sizzling electricity and smell the burning flesh of bad guys, smile, and go back to sleep. A year or so later even that whole fantasy became funny to me. I believe it was James Thurber who said, "Humor is emotional chaos remembered in tranquility."

Here is the principle that I have come to through all of this: if a thing is going to be funny in a year or two, it's probably funny now. So why wait. Laugh about it now. The gods really zeroed in on you this time and assembled an obstacle course of mishaps for you to stumble through, all for their enjoyment. Sometimes you will insist "the gods must be crazy" (to borrow a wonderful movie title). Just remember, it's all a joke, and it's on you. Viewed from the perspective of eternity, that whole tragic, ridiculous roller coaster we call life will probably look pretty trivial. So laugh about it now. You suffered through it, why not derive the benefit from it? Even the worst day of your life can help you on your way to becoming beautiful from the inside out.

Television and radio are a whole different world from the hours of about 2 A.M. to 5 A.M. A whole different cast of gremlins takes over the studios, and the things they send over the air waves are amazing. On one sleepless night I caught one of those old movies that can only be seen at 3 A.M. There were a bunch of Greek gods gathered around what appeared to be a California hot tub. In the tub was a toy ship. One of the gods began to swirl the water with his hands while another blew on the ship creating a little storm. They all smiled. Then the camera began to pan in on the ship to reveal that it was in fact a real ship in a real storm. It was a real ocean and the real people on board the ship were in desperate fear of their lives. No one was smiling. We take our storms and our lives so seriously. Perhaps if we would try to see our silly selves from the perspective of eternity, we could smile, knowing that what we call storms are only little swirls in God's hot tub.

Jesus often smiled at His disciples for taking themselves so seriously. In the sixth chapter of Matthew, He chides them for their nervous anxiety. He says, "Don't be anxious about things like food and clothing. Look at the flowers and the birds how God takes care of them. Unless you don't think you are as important as a sparrow, your worrying is silly." Jesus would have liked Bobby McFerrin's song "Don't Worry, Be Happy!"

Ministers are sometimes asked about their favorite Bible verse. Mine is a bit unusual I suppose: Luke 12:32: "Fear not, little flock, for it is your Father's good pleasure to give you the kingdom." Can't you hear the whimsy in Jesus' voice and see the twinkle in His eye as He almost teases His serious-minded disciples? Don't worry so much, He tells them. The kingdom is yours. God is going to give it to you just because He wants to.

This was spoken to people who had been struggling to achieve the kingdom throughout their whole lives and were part of a race of people who had been struggling for the same kingdom for centuries. They prayed for it, fasted for it, disciplined themselves for it. They agonized over the keeping of the Law and pleasing God, always falling short of the goal. The kingdom was always just beyond their grasp. Then along comes Jesus with a little chuckle in His voice announcing that the kingdom is God's gift, so don't take yourself too seriously.

Striving for the kingdom would be like working your whole life to make enough money to buy a Porsche 911SC only to discover that every time you neared the goal the price went up. Finally, in your senior years, when you are about to resign yourself to the prospect that the most sought after of all possessions will always be just beyond your grasp, a smiling prophet comes by and tells you it's parked in your driveway. What was all that work and worry for? Didn't you understand that your Benefactor was going to give it to you all along? Fear not little flock. Don't worry, be happy.

Though Christ employed several types of humor, the most common type He used was irony. Elton Trueblood, in his book *The Humor of Christ*, described it as "A holding up to public view of either vice or folly, but without a note of bitterness or the attempt to harm. The ironical is always marked with a subtle sharpness of insight, free from the desire to wound. This is what distinguishes it most clearly from sarcasm."

It is the irony of life situations, even tragic ones, that gives birth to humor, as illustrated in the obligatory stagecoach-being-chased-by-wild-Indians scene in the old "B" westerns. Inside the coach are several passengers, including a stereotypical preacher. He's a wimpy little man, all decked out in black, with a flat-brimmed preacher's hat and a solemn holy look about him. He does what preachers are supposed to do during times of crisis: he reads his Bible and prays. An arrow comes through the coach window, through the Bible, and into the preacher's heart. What irony, the only one hit is the one praying. The prostitute gets out without a scratch. What about all the stories we hear about Bibles stopping bullets and lives being miraculously saved? As the movie preacher slumps to the floor of the coach, a silly little smile crosses his face. At the moment of his "death," he sees the irony in it all.

Life is like that. You do everything right, and everything goes wrong. You have the Midas touch in reverse. That was precisely the source of the conflict behind the plot of the movie about Mozart, *Amadeus*. Why is the most irreverent musician blessed by God with such a great gift while the devout one (Salieri) is only mediocre? In the closing scene there is that wonderfully ironic moment where Salieri is seen as an old man in a mental institution, absolving the other patients of their mediocrity.

One of the questions that is often asked ministers is "Why do bad things happen to good people?" Harold Kushner wrote a best-selling book about that question, but nowhere in his book did he consider the answer that occurs to me at this moment. If bad things only happened to bad people and good things to good people, it wouldn't be funny. The humor of life lies in the irony.

It gets even funnier when the little setbacks start to compound themselves like an old Laurel and Hardy movie. Every move to correct an accident caused by the last move creates another "fine mess." The more paint buckets knocked over by the ladder on someone's shoulder, the funnier it gets.

There was a comical insurance claim that circulated around offices several years ago. It was probably made up, but it was just absurd enough to be credible. It was about a brick mason who finished his work and discovered that he had several dozen bricks too many on the top floor of the building. Rather than go to all the work of carrying them down, he had a bright idea. He went down and hoisted up a bucket and tied it off. He filled the bucket with the bricks and climbed back down to lower the bucket. The problem was that the bucket was now heavier than he was. So when he untied the rope, he shot up like a rocket as the bucket came down. They met at the halfway point where he sustained several injuries but managed to hang on to the rope all the way to the top. When the bucket hit the ground, some of the bricks fell out. The bucket, now being lighter than the man, started back up and he came down. They again met in the middle where he sustained more colorful injuries. When he hit the ground, landing on a pile of bricks, he let go of the rope. The bucket fell down and hit him. Is that a picture of your life sometimes? Can you find humor in it? Can you hear anyone laughing? Can you laugh with them? If you can, it's the sign of a healthy spirit.

Those comedians who find humor in the everyday events of their lives do us a great service; they help us to look for the humor in our own lives and give us permission to smile at tragedy. The stories are everywhere. The effect of the storytelling on your spirit is conditioned by whether you choose to see it as comedy or tragedy, whether the recounting of it gives you ulcers or smile lines.

Matt Weinstein, founder of Playfair Corporation, told of standing in line behind a woman at an airline ticket counter. There was some problem. Apparently the ticket had been reserved but not paid for, and she, thinking it was paid for, had no money. Finally she left the counter, and Matt stepped forward. At the gate he saw the same woman again. He casually mentioned that she had apparently gotten her ticket problem straightened out. She said that she had not and told him of her plight. Matt said he knew that one of two things was happening: either she was authentically a damsel in distress or he was being hustled. Considering himself a pretty good judge of character, he opted for the first, went back to the ticket counter with the woman and paid her fare, $120 for a one-way ticket to Dallas. They had a lovely conversation on the plane, exchanged phone numbers, and she promised to call him on Monday to make arrangements to repay the debt. Monday came—no phone call. Tuesday—no call. On Wednesday he decided to call the number she had given him. He was relieved when the voice answered "Texas Instruments," because that is where she said she worked. He asked for her by name. They had never heard of her.

Matt said his first impulse was to take a six-month leave of absence from his job and track her down. Then he thought about it again. This is what he said: "I realized that I had witnessed one of the finest theatrical performances of all time. I don't usually pay $120 for a theater ticket, but I don't usually get to sit that close either." Then he added, "Being a public speaker, I have told that story about a thousand times, and by now I figure I owe her money." How wise of him to look at it that way.

Most people have about the same amount of troubles. Some people take them one at a time in manageable doses, laugh, and move on. Others let them pile up until the heap is insurmountable. Humor is one of the best ways to put a finality to things, to diffuse potentially explosive situations, and to take a breath and then move on.

My wife and I had one of those arguments once, the kind where you forget what the original issue is, but the tension hangs in the air for days. We had been living in a state of alienation for about two weeks. It was Monday night, volleyball night, at the YMCA. She went for a hard serve, and the ball came up off her hands and hit her in the forehead. I made a crack like, "That's using your head." I knew it was a poorly timed remark the instant the words crossed my lips, but the damage was done. She was furious. Making no attempt to hide her rage, she left the gym prepared to walk the five or six miles home. I got the car, caught up with her and coaxed her in. Then we drove in silence, not to our house, but to the beach, where I pulled her out of the car and threw her into the ocean. I told her if she didn't shape up I was going to hold her under next time. She began to laugh (thank God), and we rolled around in the surf, covering ourselves with sand and seaweed. We were a mess, but the tension was gone. Humor is a miracle worker.

Remember when you were a child and your dad would say, "I see a smile coming . . ."? Try as hard as you could, you could not keep from smiling. It's impossible to keep a "good" mad on if you are smiling. Humor can rescue situations that a year of therapy won't touch. The next time you and your spouse have an argument, get a couple of water pistols and go at it. Instead of inviting one another to fight, invite one another to come out and play.

One of the major problems confronting psychotherapists and counselors is depression. Everyone seems to have some, and there are tons of paperbacks on the bookstore shelves dealing with it. They are mostly "how to" books: how to get out of a depression when you are in it. A certain amount of depression, however, is normal, even healthy. It becomes unhealthy when it goes on for long periods of time. Depression is a tool. It prompts a certain amount of introspection and triggers positive change as a result. Someone asked Paul Simon why his songs were mostly about sad themes, was he a sad person? He said that he was seldom depressed; it was just that he was more creative when he was depressed so that was when he wrote most of his songs.

Note that I am not speaking here about long-term clinical depressions. That kind of depression is very dangerous. A person suffering from it should call a professional and get help immediately.

When it is the occasional, common, normal kind of depression that can be creative, I recommend that people, rather than trying to get rid of it, play with it a little. You wake up in the morning. It's a gray, rainy Monday. You say to yourself, "Boy, am I depressed!" Maybe it's one of those days when your hair won't go right. You are off on a good depression, so play into it. Go into your closet, to the back of the closet where you put all those clothes that you hate—those things that you bought because they looked good on you in the store, but by the time you got them home they had turned major league ugly. You can't throw them away because you paid so much for them. You can't give them to the Salvation Army because they are like new. Clothes you hate will never wear out. Dress yourself in those clothes and go look at yourself in the mirror again.

Now you are really depressed. So you go down to one of those awful restaurants, one where all the waitresses are named Mabel. They call you "Honey" and yell your order to the kitchen. You order slimy eggs, extra fat bacon, a double shot of grease on your hash browns, and wash it all down with a cup of cold black coffee with a bug in the bottom. You get back to your car and discover that a pigeon has made a deposit on your windshield. If you aren't laughing by now, there's something wrong with you. Remember an abnormal reaction to an abnormal situation is normal. Lighten up! Life is a joke, and it's on you.

Ministers are some of the worst when it comes to taking themselves too seriously. After all, we are the ones charged with the task of rescuing souls from the fires of hell—a heavy responsibility. What a tragedy if we would relax a little and miss one. Some ministers work eighty hours a week in order to be true to their calling. But we have to set reasonable limits, as important as the job is. There are two rules by which I govern myself as a minister. (1) About 90 percent of the problems that arise in the church will go away if you ignore them. (2) The Kingdom of God does not rise or fall depending upon how well I do today. Those ministers who put in eighty hours a week may seem more dedicated than I, but I'll be working at it long after they have burned out. Perhaps the point of this whole chapter is this, "He who laughs, lasts."

Life is play. It's an intricate board game. It contains a certain amount of surprise, joy, depression, grief, adventure, and tragedy. A healthy, beautiful spirit responds with a smile of anticipation when the doorbell rings and a voice from the cosmos invites you to come out and play.

Remember that life is play. Most of the things that happen to you would be funny if they happened to a stand-up comedian. Don't take yourself so seriously. If a thing is going to be funny someday, it's funny now. Use humor to defuse tension and wipe away depression. Imagine how God must be smiling at you, and smile with Him.

4

I AM!

Moses was walking on a mountainside one day. This was a familiar path, one he knew well for he had tended sheep in that region for the past forty years. But on this ordinary day he saw something he had never seen before: a burning bush. The burning bush was not unusual; what was unusual was the fact that though it was burning the bush was not being consumed by the flames. Moses went to take a closer look and stopped suddenly when a voice spoke to him from the bush, commanding him to take off his shoes out of reverence for the place upon which he stood.

Wherever God meets with humans, that place is designated as holy ground. In the conversation that followed Moses was so bold as to ask the divine voice its name, and the voice answered, "I Am!" Moses didn't ask any more questions because he recognized that name; it was also his name—and it's yours and mine. When God breathed into us all the breath of life through Adam He breathed into us something of Himself; that something being pure identity. Thus our mutual creed, our common statement of faith is "I Am!"

How can you have a sense of purpose about yourself in a world that numbers its people in the billions? We are in a world where even the statistics of life and death are too enormous to be personal and are often the subject of jokes because of their irrelevance. Did you hear about the couple with four children who decided not to have any more because they had heard that every fifth child born in the world was Chinese?

You know how statistics go. In the time that it will take you to read this paragraph, as many people as would equal the population of a major American city have shuffled off the world scene, and no one even noticed. In the same period of time another city full of babies has been born, most of whom we will never meet and who will never even hear of our existence. How can you feel any sense of identity in a world like that? I read recently that someone is murdered in the United States every twenty-seven minutes. Yet most of us will never know one of those persons or be one. The brutalizing statistics of the multitudes have relegated the individual to a blip on a screen, a byte on a computer disk. We are a speck in the liquid that covers the eye of God—one blink and we are gone and no one notices. How can you find identity and purpose in a world like that?

It matters that you believe that it matters that you lived; it matters because it will change the way you live. You are an absolutely unique being in all of God's creation. In all the eons of recorded and unrecorded history, there has never been anyone quite like you, nor will the world see the likes of you again after you are gone. You are a prototype for whom the blueprints have been lost. You are created in the image of God, endowed with all kinds of divine attributes and set free to be, to build, to destroy, to love, to hate, to grow, and to die. What an adventure! The healthy spirit is the one who says: "It matters that I have lived. I will make my mark in the world. This will be a different place for my having been here."

There is a scene in *Ben Hur* where Charlton Heston is chained to an oar of a slave ship. He clings to a confidence that the time will come when he will be free again. His Roman captor scoffs at the idea. The slave says, "There must be some reason why God has kept me alive these two years." The Roman responds, "That's the trouble with you Hebrews, always insisting that life has meaning." That's a marvelous analysis of the Jewish people; they always insist that their life as individuals and particularly as a people, a race, has meaning. The value that they place on their own existence no doubt accounts for their continued existence. What nation can exist without a homeland for two thousand years? What ethnic group can exist over the centuries dispersed all over the world and absorbed by its cultures? Yet the Jews have maintained their identity because they believed it mattered that they do so. Life has purpose; life has meaning.

We Christians follow in that grand tradition. We are a people who believe not only that all people are created in God's image, but that God loves us individually, redeemed us by name, and has a purpose for our lives, each life.

Viktor Frankl, to whom I referred earlier, said that he was able to survive his death camp experience simply because of the knowledge that he had choices and that those choices mattered. He had no choice about where he was, what he did, what he ate, or whether he lived or died, but he had a choice about his attitude. He could choose daily how he would feel about the guard who struck him or how he would respond to those who treated him cruelly and held his life in their hands. He had a choice that mattered, and it saved his life. It mattered to him that he live, so he lived.

I believe that the everyday choices you make change the world; that doesn't mean that you will become famous for it. Famous people are not necessarily the ones who change the world; they just get lots of press. The world is not changed so much by generals, bankers, and politicians as it is by housewives, poets, and the farmer-philosophers. The change they initiate is slower and anonymous, but it grinds on where flashier movements that catch the attention of headline writers sputter and fail.

Israel Goldstein has written, "I believe that greatness is not synonymous with prominence, and that the most meaningful kind of earthly immortality is that of commitment to human enterprises that live on after us." Activities to which we give ourselves which in turn give us meaning and purpose can be subtle and simple and even common. There are some people whom I think of as great, but you have never heard of most of them; they are great in my eyes because they touch other people in life-changing ways. I came across the following poem:

> Hurrah for those who never invented anything;
> Hurrah for those who never explored anything;
> Hurrah for those who never conquered anything;
> But who, in awe, gave themselves up to the essence of
>   things,
> Ignorant of the shell, but seized by the rhythm of things,
> Not intent on conquest, but playing the play of the world.

That's my definition of a great person. It's not a matter of what they do but how they live. They understand that the value of things has no relationship to their cost nor does their importance bear any relationship to their newsworthiness. It has been said that Andy Warhol collected both antiques and junk together in one collection. He searched for meaning in fine art stores and second-hand stores. It was said, "He saw the beauty in things regardless of price."

It matters how we live because our every action affects other people and other people make up society and the values of the society control and change the world. So you are important because your smallest actions have the potential to change the world. Yes, even the little things.

"Go ahead, make my day" was popularized in a Dirty Harry movie and shall live on in infamy. Of course Harry meant it in a rather sinister way, but I believe that nothing adds purpose to life quite like making someone's day. It becomes especially challenging and fun if you are in a place where people don't want or expect to have their day made. A formidable challenge might be a stereotypically rude waiter in a New York restaurant.

Perhaps every city has one thing about it that the conscientious tourist absolutely must take in so as to have experienced the city genuinely. Los Angeles has movie studios; San Francisco, the bridge. When you are in Chicago, you go to the Loop; Washington, the Smithsonian; and when in Boston, you walk the Freedom Trail and visit the "Cheers" bar.

In New York you go to an overpriced restaurant to be insulted by a rude waiter. On my visit to the Big Apple my friend assured me that this was a favorite pastime of locals and tourists alike. Some of the more popular restaurants had a two-hour waiting list after which you might never even see a waiter except when he appeared to receive his tip, which he expected to be in double digits since the check was in triple digits. It was very New York!

On my first full day in the city we walked the short distance from my friend's office to a lunch place he assured me was one of those "happening" places. "It's very New York," he asserted as he confidently led the way.

It was one of those bitter cold days in New York, one that was too cold to snow, the kind of cold that's hard for a Southern Californian to imagine when he is packing his suitcase with all the warm things from the bottom dresser drawer: sweaters, a wool coat, and, yes, even fur-lined gloves. My suitcase now lay empty on a New York bedroom floor as I had taken the "layered look" to a ridiculous extreme. As if to prove a point, when I rounded the corner at Forty-Second Street, the New York chill cut mercilessly through all my Southern California garments, making the whole dressing ritual meaningless. I didn't talk any more; my face had grown stiff. It was just as well because the last three things I had said were nothing but futile attempts at some comparison between the cold that I had known and the cold I was now experiencing.

We thankfully made it to the restaurant. It was decorated in a fifties motif with a big Rock-ola jukebox by the front door blasting out old Fats Domino hits in incomparable monophonic high fidelity. It was very New York, indeed, but I was looking past the decor, hoping to find a place near a heat vent. As my eyes scanned the walls, I heard the voice of the hostess say in a crisp monotone, "May I help you?" She was a lovely, plump black woman who looked remarkably like the nanny from *Gone with the Wind*. I found myself lusting for her body heat, and without considering where I was I responded, "Yes, you can give me a big hug and warm me up." A broad smile broke over her face as she extended her arms to me and we indulged in a full-body embrace, unrestrained and warm. Then she led us to a table away from the drafts of the front door.

That evening I was out to eat again with my friend and his wife. The restaurant was very French *and* very New York. The maître d' reluctantly handed us the menus, making sure that we had to extend our arms full length to reach them. His demeanor and that of the waiter who finally arrived steered our conversation again toward the notoriety of rude New York restaurants. Whereupon my friend said to his wife, "You won't believe what happened at lunch today." He told the story of the impromptu restaurant hug and then added, "My coffee cup was always full, the food was prompt; in fact, in all the times I've been to that restaurant, I've never received that kind of service."

I had made her day and perhaps had sown a seed that would lead to the transformation of New York City. Perhaps one day New York will be known as a city of friendly waiters and waitresses and maître d's who hug their patrons. Of course no one will give me credit for it—no one will know it was I who started it all with one little hug—but I will know and I will smile down from my vantage point on some eternal perch. The anticipation of the long-range outcome of my actions gives me a sense of meaning and purpose even now.

And finally it is impossible to speak of meaning and purpose without speaking of love. Nothing is quite so effective at creating a sense of identity and value in a person as being the object or source of real love and affection.

Years ago Nat King Cole crooned the words to a song called "Nature Boy":

> There was a boy, a very strange enchanted boy,
> As he spoke of many things
> fools and kings
> This he said to me.
> The greatest thing you will ever learn
> Is just to love
> And be loved in return.

And the disciple whom Jesus loved has written: "Love is of God, and he who loves is born of God and knows God" (1 John 4:7). To love is to know and be known by God, to be at one with the One who first said "I Am" and who calls forth that unique identity in each of us.

John Powell, in his book *Through Seasons of the Heart*, said this of that love that gives meaning and sets free:

> A sense of his or her own worth is no doubt the greatest gift we can offer to another, the greatest contribution we can make to any life. We can give this gift and make this contribution only through love. However, it is essential that our love be liberating, not possessive. We must at all times give those we love the freedom to be themselves. Love affirms the other as other. It does not possess and manipulate another as "mine." Pertinent here is the quotation of Frederick Perls: "You did not come into this world to live up to my expectations. And I did not come into the world to live up to yours. If we meet it will be beautiful. If we don't it can't be helped."
>
> To love is to liberate. Love and friendship must empower those we love to become their best selves, according to their own lights and visions. This means that wanting what is best for you and trying to be what you need me to be can be done only in a way that preserves your freedom to have your own feelings, think your own thoughts and make your own decisions. If your personhood is as dear to me as my own, which is the implication of love, I must respect it carefully and sensitively. When I affirm you, my affirmation is based on your unconditional value as a unique, unrepeatable and even sacred mystery of humanity.

Every day we make choices that change the world. It may not seem that way; most of us will never do great things or become famous. Our deaths won't merit too many lines in the local newspaper, but it matters that we live, and we must live our lives as if we were front-page news. It matters for two reasons. First, because somewhere out there are the persons who taught Albert Einstein and Adolf Hitler, who started them on the paths they eventually followed to their conclusions. As children, they probably seemed very much alike, indeed they were much like typical European boys. But some anonymous someone who didn't know how much it mattered touched those lives, and they changed the world. Someone taught Abraham Lincoln about honesty and perseverance. Someone taught Charles Manson about the value of human life. There are people who dreamed the dreams that long after their unannounced deaths became the Space Shuttle, the Olympic Games, the cure for smallpox, the United States of America. You may be the one who touches the life that touches the world, the discoverer of the cure for cancer, the designer of the treaty that eliminates nuclear weapons.

In the Bible that someone was Andrew. Andrew was Peter's brother and is always identified as such in the Scriptures. That's because Peter went on to become the superstar, one of the Big Three disciples, chief of the apostles, and prince of the church. The biggest church in the world is named in honor of Peter. Perhaps the only thing Andrew ever did of any real significance was to introduce his brother to Jesus, and the rest, as they say, is history. The unheralded Andrews of the world make all the difference.

It matters, second, because if you believe it matters, it will make a difference in how you live, how carefully you plan, how high you reach, what sort of person you become. Live life with a purpose. Love, share, teach, and give as if everything depended on it because ultimately it does.

There is a graffiti wall somewhere in South Philadelphia. Big angry slogans are written all over it with spray paint. There are expletives and threats and obscene drawings. There is gang language written in some code that can't mask the anger and violence behind it. If we move closer, we see that in the mortar between the bricks someone has written with a felt pen in a fine hand "I Am."

It's the most profound message on the wall; it is the name by which we are all called, it is our family name given to us as a heritage from our Father.

- Live your life as if it had meaning and purpose.
- Find meaning through making someone else's day, through teaching, and by loving and being loved.
- Remember that how you feel about yourself changes your behavior and your behavior changes the world.

5

Incongruity, Ambiguity, Paradox, Irony, and Rebellion

This chapter title sounds a little like the name of a law firm. I can just see it printed in gold letters on some mahogany door somewhere: "The Offices of Incongruity, Ambiguity, Paradox, Irony, and Rebellion, Inc." On second thought it sounds not so much like a law firm as an "outlaw" firm. These are the words that call forth the Jesse James in all of us.

From time to time we have to visit these offices if our spirits are to be freed from stagnation and grow to be healthy and beautiful. These are the words that fly in the face of organization and frustrate efforts to simplify, explain, pacify, domesticate, and organize our lives. All of us need some organization in our lives, of course, but the structuring of life must be an ongoing process. If this structuring process ever arrives at a conclusion, if these organizing efforts are ever completely successful, then the results would be deadly. Loose ends sense the rhythm of life better than those that are neatly tucked in.

Healthy spirits must avoid the trap of perfect structure—all the pegs being in the right holes, all questions answered, all problems solved. A seminary professor told me that the task of a graduate education was not to give answers but to give better questions. He went on to say, "Every door of knowledge I open, opens on a room full of ignorance." And someone has whimsically quipped,

43

"I want to announce an alarming increase in the number of things about which I know nothing."

Healthy spirits need fuzzy edges, contradictory information, definitions that don't work, and mutually exclusive facts. Healthy spirits need to disagree for the fun of it and take the road less traveled simply because it is the road less traveled. Real-life adventure comes out of the hodgepodge of loose ends and inconclusive conclusions. So we may work our whole life to organize things, answer questions, align our ducks, and arrive at orderliness, but let us pray that we never succeed.

I read an article some time ago entitled "What If the Dream Came True?" It was based on a study of an upper-middle-class neighborhood in Michigan populated by people whose goal was the American dream (a company or bank presidency, a lovely suburban ranch-style home, a lovely wife, a handsome husband, 2.4 healthy children, and memberships in the country club, the Republican party, and a white steepled church).

What made the article so interesting to me was that these people had all accomplished their dreams. They were middle aged and they had achieved their goals. Now they were bored to death. What do you do when you feel that life is over when your life is only half over? They needed to visit the outlaw offices of Incongruity, Ambiguity, Paradox, Irony, and Rebellion and shake up their lives a little bit. They needed to add a dash of contradiction, conflict, doubt, and even threat.

I have made two major geographical moves involving job changes in the past twelve years, both for the same reason: things were going too well. In 1978 I owned a lovely home in Fullerton, California. I was making a living from concert tours. I was surrounded by friends and always had one or more romances in the works. It was wonderful. I was happy, and the months and years slid by with unnoticed ease. I had my life together. I had no challenges, no threats, no big questions. So I moved! I just picked up my idyllic life and plunked it down in the lap of uncertainty. I went to San Diego, bought a house with a leaky roof in a neighborhood that I didn't like, left all my friends and romances, and took a job in a church doing something I had never done before and wasn't sure I wanted to do anyhow. The first thing I noticed was that my phone never rang and people didn't stop by. I was alone, frightened, unsure, and fearful of failure. It was exhilarating and I never looked back.

Ten years later I was in a better house in a better neighborhood. I had narrowed my romantic interests to one woman whom I subsequently married. I had lots of friends. My phone rang all the time. And I was considered by many to be an expert in the area of ministry to singles. I was happy. The years slid by with comfortable ease. So I moved and never looked back. Uncertainty is the stuff of life.

Uncertainty is also the stuff of religious faith. We defined faith earlier as holding convictions in areas where final demonstration is not possible. That means that faith by definition must include some elements of skepticism. Doubt is a necessary ingredient of faith! Some would find that last statement incongruous. They are right. Unless one can embrace a certain amount of inconsistency, it is impossible, by this definition, to have faith. For that reason the churches that offer certainty never interested me very much. There are plenty of them around who will give you all the right answers neatly packaged in a full-color brochure. They will tell you which Scriptures to read and what prayers to say. In moments it's all settled. I don't thrive on easy answers but on relevant questions worth the struggle. Religion is mystery and mystery is paradoxical ambiguity.

For example, here's a question that comes up from time to time in religious gatherings. If Jesus is the truth, the way, and the life and no man comes to the Father but by Him, then what about the person running around barefoot in a jungle somewhere who has never heard of Jesus? He doesn't have a chance and that isn't fair. Don't we believe that God is fair? And suppose we were able to communicate to him that Christ came to forgive him of his sin only to discover that in his culture there is no concept of sin. Must we teach him to be a sinner before he can then be saved? There is more than a little conflict here. A God who is all powerful and all good would not let the jungle dweller perish. If he is lost, it must be either because God is not all powerful and is unable to save him or God is not all good and doesn't want to save him. Or perhaps we just don't understand what that passage from

Scripture really means, or perhaps the person who wrote it didn't take the barefoot jungle dweller into consideration.

This question will never be answered. But its very complexity and incongruity makes it exhilarating. Truth is most likely to be found not in answers but in the struggle toward answers. In *The Different Drum*, Scott Peck says that ambiguity is frustrating for our society because it not only implies not knowing but not being able to know; therefore, "those who seek certainty, or who claim certainty in their knowledge, cannot tolerate ambiguity. . . . So it is that mystics of all cultures and religions speak in terms of paradox, not in terms of 'either/or' but in terms of 'both/and.'"

I came across an article by Ralph Wood in the *Christian Century* titled "God's Terrifying Mercy." The paradox is in the title. It was an article that I had to read. Note the emphasis on incongruity and paradox in these two quotes:

> What shall we do with something as dreadful as divine grace? . . . It is fearful to fall into the hands of God who condemns us by exoneration, who imprisons us by flinging wide the cell door, who enslaves us in the service which is perfect freedom. . . .
>
> Christ's forgiveness is what truly scandalizes us. We can explain his condemnation, but his pardon permits no pretext. To receive the miracle of God's grace is to be robbed of all defenses, shriven of all excuses. Our only recourse is to rejoice, to give thanks, and to get on with the wondrous, ordinary business of living.

This writer is on the journey toward a healthy and beautiful spirit.

To embrace unsettling concepts and unanswerable questions is as difficult as welcoming uncertainty in all of life: new jobs, new relationships, moving. It's all so painful, as indeed it should be, but it gets easier with practice. Do you remember your first love, how you thought you would die when it was over—but you didn't? That's a learning experience. When the next love relationship ended sadly, the pain was just as real, but it was a little easier on you because you had been through it before. You knew that you weren't going to die; you knew that in time it would get better.

My house in Fullerton was the hardest to leave because it was my first house. In a way it was like a first love; it was exactly what I wanted. The realtor called on a rainy Tuesday morning and said,

"I've found the house for you." I said, "But it's raining." She said, "That's why we will get there first." It was the only house I looked at. It was just right. I made the offer that day and moved in ninety days later. Over the next five years I turned that house into a gigantic art project. I built patio roofs and brick decks. I scraped, painted, and papered and even did a patchwork carpet for the living room. My thumb print was on every nail and board in that house. It was really mine.

When I decided to sell and move, I gave a party, a farewell party for my friends to say goodbye, not to me but to the house. It had become an important place for many of them as well. Several of them lamented that they couldn't imagine how I could leave the house. It had so much of me in it; my personality was all over it. At the end of the party, I made a little speech. This is how my speech went: "This house doesn't define me. I define it. This house is wonderful because I live here. When the house and I separate, it will be the house, not me, who is diminished."

The house has never recovered from the loss of me, so my old neighbors report. The irony is that in leaving the things that I loved I was made stronger. If I had stayed too long, the house might have begun to define me, and my spiritual well-being could not tolerate that. So I embraced a painful change and swallowed the giant lump that came to my throat when the "For Sale" sign went up in the front yard. In *The Different Drum*, Scott Peck says, "True adults are those of us who have learned to continually develop and exercise their capacity for transformation."

Both/And

Earlier I suggested that we should see life as play, develop a sense of humor about ourselves, and not take ourselves too seriously. I also suggested that a strong sense of purpose is essential to a healthy spirit and that we should take ourselves and our uniquenesses very seriously. These two pieces of advice could be seen as mutually exclusive. Which is correct? Both are. They both bear their own truth regardless of whether they seem to conflict with one another. Why can't there be more than one right answer? If both are good ideas, why not simply ignore the fact that they are contradictory and just embrace both. Healthy spirits must be willing to receive mutually exclusive pieces of information with glee rather than consternation.

Scientists have proven that neither the hummingbird nor the bumblebee can fly. Their flight would defy existing laws of aerodynamics. So do we abandon the laws of aerodynamics, or do we assume that some other creature is responsible for draining the nectar out of our hummingbird feeders? We do neither. We look at the contradiction, celebrate it, and smile at the wonder that is Nature. We've all heard the maxim that laws were made to be broken; maybe God said it first.

To be a spiritual person you must learn, as Scott Peck said in *The Different Drum*, "to be a 'both/and' person rather than an 'either/or' person." Jesus is an excellent model for us. He answered *yes* to the question of whether we should pay taxes to Caesar or give our offerings to God. Is the kingdom coming in the future, or is it here now? Jesus said *both*. Should we obey the law or do what the given situation suggests. *Yes.* Does conduct matter, or are we saved by grace? *Yes.* If everything in life has to fit into our neat little categories, we are going to have to leave out a lot of things. What are you going to do with the good stuff that doesn't seem to fit anywhere? Being outside our particular frame of reference makes it no less valuable. Being in direct conflict with something we hold to be true makes it no less true. Does water expand when it is frozen, or does it contract? *Both.* Open a file in your mind under the heading of "Miscellaneous." My miscellaneous file has very quickly become the largest in my filing cabinet and certainly the most interesting.

From the Miscellaneous File

Incongruity, ambiguity, paradox, irony, and rebellion—I have intentionally not defined these terms because to do so is to domesticate them and rob them of their outlaw quality. I merely share here some stories and situations from my miscellaneous file that lift them up as virtues rather than vices. Yes, even rebellion!

I never wanted to be like my parents. I never liked the way they dealt with one another: the game playing, the things they focused on as important, their colloquial, down-home way of looking at life. I suppose one of the things that encouraged me to stay single as long as I did was the fear that my marriage would be like theirs. It wasn't that there was anything particularly wrong with their relationship; it just wasn't what I wanted. By most measuring rods theirs is a good marriage, it has celebrated a duration of fifty years. They have blended into one another until it's hard to tell where one leaves off and the other begins. Their need for each other's company goes beyond companionship, friendship, and intimacy to something like life sustenance. They seem to draw their life from one another. It is lovely to behold, but it is theirs, not mine. That is rebellion speaking.

I always wanted "different" even if it wasn't necessarily "better." To this day when I am with my parents, I notice the ways in which I am like them and grimace a little. I'm starting to talk like my dad. I not only got his nose but his speech cadence also. I'm starting to see their moods and mine as mirror images. I have to change. I have to be me. That need to differentiate from parents is not uniquely mine. I didn't discover it. It is universal. That rebellion is good. It's what moves us on to new things. Birds push their young out of the nest, and some of us humans throw ourselves out of the nest whether we can fly or not. Unlike birds, we have the capacity to change our plumage, so we often distinguish ourselves from our parents by the way in which we adorn ourselves. Where my dad arranged his hair with vast quantities of Wildroot Cream Oil, I invented the dry look. My unconstrained and unruly hair was the subject of many a conversation at the supper table. Other nights we discussed my tight jeans and my loose, inside-out sweatshirt. The rebellion of my wardrobe continued through my college and seminary years.

Uniforms

I was the first guy in Dayton, Ohio, with a Nehru jacket. One night I wore it to a George Wallace political rally, and a group of about a dozen or so security guards came to search me. There were about ten thousand people in the auditorium, but I was the only one searched. When I sat down, no one would sit near me. When George came out to make his speech, there was a big empty space right in front at the podium with me sitting right in the middle of it. I was outwardly indignant, of course. Why would they assume, simply because of my dress and my long hair, that I was dangerous? Inwardly, however, I was pleased. They had noticed that I wasn't like them, and that was my intent.

The paradoxical irony is, of course, that all dress is a type of uniform. My nonconformist garb was precisely what nonconformists were supposed to be wearing in the late sixties. I bought my Nehru jacket in the nonconformist department of Neiman-Marcus. The question is begged whether there is any such thing as nonconformity or only choices as to our particular brand of conformity. We are all conformists choosing our pack and then pointing an accusing finger at those who run with other packs: preppies, yuppies, skinheads, bikers, cowboys, executives, and so on. In trying to be different, we join others who are trying to be different and in doing so uncover the stark reality that we are all similar. So in our struggle to define ourselves as unique personages, we join ranks with others engaged in the same compulsive, neurotic quest, never allowing the thought to occur to us that our parents before us involved themselves in that same self-defeating process which shaped them like they are.

Rebellion only works as a liberating influence on the spirit when it is not so much a neurotic quest as it is a natural process. The real nonconformists are the ones who are just free enough to be who they are. The real free spirits never point to their uniqueness or apologize for it because they don't realize it is there. Pure nonconformity may be like humility in that once you realize you have it, it's gone.

I had a favorite professor in seminary who invited me over to his house for dinner. It was one of those old Victorian houses in the northern suburbs of Dayton, solidly built in the 1930s with charm and character that got richer with each passing decade. The outside was elegant, the inside was a surprise. It was littered with books, magazines, papers, and junk. The stuff was stacked everywhere—end tables, coffee tables, doorways. I had to scoot some stuff over to find a place to sit on the sofa. Mind you, this was not a surprise visit, I was there by invitation. They had had a week to plan for my arrival. Here's the point. There was no apology or explanation for the mess in the house. It was never mentioned or alluded to in any way. It was their house, their lifestyle. Apparently it never occurred to them that it was extreme by most standards (even mine, which tend to be a little on the messy side). They were an example of true nonconformity and liberation. In establishing their personal priorities, housekeeping got a lower slot than most people give it. It was done not as a protest but as an expression of themselves. True liberation is not something you work for but something you have or rather something you are. Ultimately, after we are out of the nest and flying on our own, our identities must be formed not by a rejection of what others are but as an affirmation of what we are.

I grew up in my parents' home where no speck of dust was allowed to enter. We always came in the back door and took our shoes off. When I got my own home, I got two big hairy dogs and invited them to sit on the couch. That was rebellion, rejection of the values of others. In affirming my own values I have become more moderate. I am down to one big hairy dog who stays on the floor.

We celebrate that rebellious quality in those we choose as our heroes. Movies love to feature free-spirited, slightly eccentric nonconformists who move through life with a different set of expectations and rules than do the rest of us. Hollywood loves to show them to us because we love to embrace them. Every cop movie ever made has been about a cop who didn't work well with "the system." They always throw out the book and improvise, relying on snap judgment and spontaneity. Indiana Jones was asked what his plan was for retrieving the ark. "Plan," he muttered, "what plan? I'm making this up as I go!" Both Frank Sinatra and Elvis Presley used these lyrics as part of their musical biographical statement: "The record shows, I took the blows, and did it my way."

Elvis, one of the most popular and sought after people in the world, was also one of the loneliest. How can that be? Like all of

us, his life was a bundle of contradictions. As Kris Kristofferson
wrote:

> He's a walking contradiction,
> Partly truth and partly fiction,
> Taking every wrong direction
> On his lonely way back home.

We who would do life successfully and live a life that is rich and
complete are going to have to acknowledge and be comforted
with the fact that each of us is a walking contradiction. It's true
now and it always has been. Jacob the patriarch, whose name was
changed to Israel, was all his life a swindler and a flimflam man.
Moses the lawgiver was a murderer. David, the greatest king Israel
ever had, was both a murderer and an adulterer. The Bible is filled
with stories about people trying to find their way back home and
taking every wrong direction while they are at it.

Contradictions

The people of the Bible are walking contradictions as is the
book itself. Some people bristle when you suggest that the Bible
contains contradictions. They think the fact that it contradicts
itself calls into question its truth. In fact the opposite is so. Were
it not contradictory, it could not adequately reflect real life and
would thus be no longer relevant. Its incongruity and paradox are
precisely the reasons why twenty centuries after its completion
people still read it and find themselves mirrored in it. Styles
change, customs change, languages change, but that one thing
remains unchanged: the unpredictability of life and the human
spirit. It is precisely that issue that the Bible addresses. The Bible
speaks of life and death, joy and sorrow, laughter and suffering,
and judgment and mercy, all in the same divine breath. Is it any
wonder we created beings are walking contradictions? We were
created by one whose all-knowing mind sees opposite ends of any
continuum as necessary ingredients of one another. There are no
irreconcilable contradictions, only unsolved mysteries.

I wonder why it is that I, someone who loves and indeed
craves solitude, also hungers for togetherness? Can the need to

be in community and the need to be alone be mysterious expressions of the same need, possibly the need to be?

I believe it was Leonardo da Vinci who said, "When you are with a friend, you share everything, but when you are alone, everything is yours." I believe that. Yet in those times when everything is truly mine, meaning tends to be lost for lack of someone with whom to share it. I wonder what my Walden experience (to which I shall refer later) would have been like if the whole thing had been shared with another person. I suspect that a good deal of its richness remains because it was an experience lived in solitude, but even as I say that, I wish that there had been someone with whom I could reflect on that time on the farm, someone who was there.

Why would an introvert like myself choose what many consider to be an extrovert's career? Both performing and ministry require an outgoing, people-oriented personality. Being on stage or in the pulpit is always unnatural and frightening. Still I crave it as I crave the opportunities for complete withdrawal. My chosen profession is the cause of my greatest joy and deepest anxiety. It is the source of both the agony and the ecstasy of my life.

Introvert

It came as something of a surprise to me to discover that I was an introvert. I suppose I always knew it down deep, but to have the condition named and to see it printed out on a clinical test form was a bit of a shock. I was at a lecture series at the University of Wisconsin when I was given the opportunity to take the Myers-Briggs personality inventory. What did I have to lose? They assured me that it was impossible to flunk a personality test. Out of twenty-eight questions that indicated an introvert tendency, I scored positive on twenty-five. What in the world was I doing then on stage singing songs or in the pulpit preaching to a congregation?

After a little more research I discovered that the words *introvert* and *extrovert* didn't mean exactly what their popular usage might imply. They aren't synonymous with words like *withdrawn* and *outgoing* but refer rather to the focus of one's adventure. For the extrovert the adventure of life is outside in the world of

experiences, relationships, interactions; for the introvert the adventure is within. The grandest mysteries and dramas are played
out in the mind and the imagination. So to be an introvert
doesn't mean that one is any less capable of relating to other
people or even being in a leadership role, it just takes more energy
for him or her. The introvert is fatigued by interaction while the
extrovert is energized by it. You can find them at parties. The
introvert says, "Let's go home, I'm tired," to which the extrovert
spouse responds, "You've got to be kidding, we just got here!"

More Questions

Why is it that we choose occupations that don't seem to match
our temperament or spouses who are our opposites? Why do we
evening people always seem to end up related to a morning person whose biorhythms are exactly opposite from ours? The answer is probably found in one of these five words: *rebellion, irony,
paradox, ambiguity,* and *incongruity.*

Why do the things we do to make ourselves happy end up only
increasing our misery? People who are unhappily single get married only to discover that instead of being happy they have succeeded in making someone else unhappy. Studies show that
people who are happily married were also happily single, or, in
other words, happiness was not the thing that caused them to
want to be married, they already had that. For those who marry
to find happiness, there is disappointment; for those happy people who marry for other reasons, happiness is multiplied. How
can that be fair? Then those two unhappy married people decide
to have a baby to make them happy, and everyone knows what
a disaster that can be. Why is it that the things that lend meaning
and substance, even happiness, to life are the things we most
vigorously avoid: commitment, suffering, self-denial? Jesus said,
"He who finds his life will lose it, and he who loses his life for my
sake will find it" (Matt. 10:39). How about that for paradox? You
could spend the rest of your life trying to figure out what that
means, and if you did the world would either call you insane or a
saint. Albert Schweitzer left a career in medicine and music, being
an acknowledged genius in both fields, and went to Africa to

minister to people who could have no appreciation of his genius. Was it a waste of life? Was he crazy? Was it just rebellion? I don't know. I only know that his life was given meaning when he introduced the elements of self-sacrifice and commitment to it. Most now call him saint, some still call him insane. In the end all that matters is what we call ourselves and how we are called by God.

When I decided to go into the ministry I was eighteen years old. I announced my intention to the pastor of my church who, though surprised and dismayed, began the process required in our Methodist book of rules. In the United Methodist Church a ministerial candidate must be recommended by his or her local church, then the district, then the conference. As part of that process I met with the district superintendent, a gentle, old, gray-haired man with a dark gray suit and a passion for poetry. He looked at me critically, shook his head, and said, "You'll never make it." "Why?" I asked. "Because, you're not the type," he answered. "That," I insisted, "is what I consider to be my strongest asset." After thirty years I'm sure I was right. Why should I be predictable when nothing else in life is? Why should I fall easily into someone else's category when no one else falls easily into categories for me?

When I am flying I often like to sleep. I have discovered that if I let the person next to me know that I am a minister that usually ends the conversation and they will leave me alone for the rest of the flight. Sometimes it doesn't work. A woman smiled and said, "That's very interesting. Tell me, do you pattern your ministry after Billy Graham or Oral Roberts?" I was not happy with the range of options given me or with the ease with which she tried to categorize me. I said, "I think of myself as more of an Elmer Gantry type." Then she left me alone and I went to sleep.

The Christmas Tree

In seminary I encountered one of the great oxymorons: systematic theology. To use the words "system" and the "study of God" in the same phrase was idiotic. God will not be confined to our systems. Just as God exists beyond the concepts of time and space, God exists beyond systems.

I think of my theology more as a Christmas tree with hundreds of colored ornaments. Each ornament is unique in size, shape, and color. Each has no relationship with the other ornaments on the tree, but there they all hang out together. These ornaments are my experiences of God that make up the way I think about Him or my theology.

A fellow seminary student had been a fighter pilot in Vietnam. He told me this story. His plane had taken some hits and was losing altitude over enemy territory. There was one mountain range standing between him and a safe landing at his home base. A glance at the altimeter and at the horizon quickly confirmed beyond doubt that he was too low. He wasn't going to make it. So he began to pray. He said, "It was like a big hand came out of the sky and lifted the plane over the mountains to safety."

What shall I do with that story? I'm a rather orthodox, yet skeptical type with not much space in my theological filing cabinet for "Big Hand" stories. If I were an either/or person, I would have to do one of two things with that story. I would either have to reject it as untrue, or I would have to adopt it as part of my theological statement and renovate my filing system to accommodate it. Being a both/and person, I have another option. I don't have to question the authenticity of the story. It's his story, not mine. He's alive to tell it, and that fact alone lends it some credibility. Nor do I have to remodel my theology to make a comfortable place for it. I just fit it into my wonderful miscellaneous file and let it rub against all the other God stories with which it is contradictory, or I just add it to my Christmas tree. I don't try to make all the ornaments match or establish a certain pattern. I just hang them there and let them reflect off one another. Every once in a while I walk by, look, and say, "Isn't that interesting?"

Once I was in a car with another minister headed into town to a particular store to pick up an item. Main Street was jammed and, as we we drove past the store, there were no parking places in sight. He said, "That's OK, we'll just pray and God will provide a parking place." Once again, my theology doesn't have a category for a divine errand boy who gets people parking places, a heavenly valet service. We drove around the block and, just as we approached the store again, a car pulled out right in front and we pulled in. Guess what I did with that story. I hung it up there on my Christmas tree, and every once in a while I walk by and say, "Isn't that interesting?"

Over the years my Christmas tree has accumulated quite an array of ornaments, each unique and fascinating in itself. In combination or in tension, they are all the more exhilarating. Now and then I walk by and let my spirit be energized by the brilliance of it all.

This life we live will not be confined or defined. It is the nature of life to always be growing and changing; always pushing our limits and challenging our perceptions. We who would dance the dance of life, embrace a light-hearted elusive partner. We who would confine life to narrow categories of our own making have nailed our own feet to the floor.

Celebrate the creative tension in your life. The friction of mutually exclusive bits of experience rubbing together in your life's filing cabinet will produce light and heat to warm the healthy spirit.

Take note of the things in your life that are unorganized, contradictory, and threatening, things that could be described as loose ends and unanswered questions. Begin to view these, not with consternation, but with joy. They don't complicate your life, they make life interesting. Without them life is not life, it is only existence.

Postscript—Walden

Henry David Thoreau exemplifies for me the kind of qualities I tried to describe in chapter 5. The more I read about him and by him, the more I feel that his was a life lived as it ought to be. Most people know him for his famous commentary about people having the right to march to a different drummer. Thoreau described himself as a mystic and a transcendental philosopher. He wrote once, "the greater part of what my neighbors call good, I believe in my soul to be bad, and if I repent of anything it is very likely to be my good behavior." How about that for rebellion!

The most engaging event in Thoreau's life for me, the one that displays the purity of his free spirit and does most to call forth in me the desire to follow, is the Walden Pond adventure: "When I wrote the following pages, or rather the bulk of them, I lived alone in the woods, a mile from any neighbor, in a house which I built myself, on the shore of Walden Pond in Concord, Massachusetts, and earned my living by the labor of my hands only." In that one introductory sentence Thoreau has put forth a myriad of images that fill me with wonder and longing and a sense of "If only I could do that." Listen to the litany of wonder:

> I lived alone
> in the woods

a mile from any neighbor
in a house which I built myself
on the shore of Walden Pond
and earned my living by the labor of my hands.

Any of these statements is the stuff of which dreams are made, at least for me. These words set my mind rushing to places and times beyond myself and fill me with visions of perfect solitude, of hard work and silent sleep, of log cabins and wood fires, and of a little garden by the pond (often raided by the other creatures of the woods). I would not be a visitor or an intruder but a part of it, a piece of the landscape, uncaring and unaware of outside life, people and their troubles, the rush of the interstate highway just over the hill, political intrigue, and wars and rumors of wars. This for me describes utopia better than anything.

I came close once, almost by accident. That's probably why I was able to come so close. If I had gone with a well-planned strategy, it probably would never have happened. The experience was almost over before I realized I was on Walden Pond.

After a year of serving a church in California, I went back to Ohio for a reunion with my seminary buddies with whom I had performed in a singing group. We were the theological school's answer to Peter, Paul, and Mary. We brought theological understanding to Paul Simon and Bob Dylan or a musical setting for Friedrich Schleiermacher and Augustine, depending on how you looked at it. We decided to regroup and hit the concert trail full time for a couple of years before we got serious and settled into our respective chosen careers. So the first item of business was to move back to Ohio and find a place to live.

The apartments around Dayton, Ohio, all looked alike and were exactly like the one I had rented in California: overpriced, Navajo white in color, and predictability reproduced in cookie-cutter fashion all up and down the landscape. Something in me cried out for something—anything—else.

I went to visit an old friend, the seminary student recruiter. We had put in some miles together in past years visiting colleges and wooing the pretheological students with my guitar and his smooth monologue. He had bought a cattle farm in the rolling countryside outside of Dayton near a little village named Brookville (that's almost as good a name as Walden Pond).

He showed me around the spacious farmhouse, the barns, and the cattle shed. Then there was the outer building where the tractors were parked. It had an upper floor that was a kind of attic. There was a sink, electricity, and some sticks of furniture—someone once lived there. He speculated that someone had turned it into living quarters during World War II and it had been all but forgotten ever since. The only inhabitants now were the mice who lived in the walls, the birds in the eaves, and the swarm of bees just outside the window that faced the barn and the cow pond.

I said, "I want to live here." We worked out a deal for $35 per month, and I would do all the renovation. I had about two months before the singing group had any serious commitments and before the rain, snow, and cold would become a factor. It was two months of sheer joy.

I moved in determined not to displace the mice, the birds, or the bees and not to insult the place by introducing any items that were new. The first piece of furniture was an old Hoosier cabinet that was given to me. I kept it for nearly twenty years before I finally sold it on consignment to an antique store. I never fully admitted to anyone how I loved that old thing. When the antique dealer asked me what I wanted to charge for it, I said that I didn't care, any amount would be more than I paid for it and much less than it was worth. The day the check came in the mail I cried.

I found a used coal oil stove for heating and a used carpet for the floor. All of the furniture was taken off a trash heap or bought dirt cheap at Denny's used furniture store. I went to see Denny often. In two months he came to know me by name. The walls were reconstructed where the mice had eaten away the wallboard, then covered with old bedsheets, funny papers, or brightly colored paint (there was no Navajo white anywhere). I put tape on the sharp edges of a broken mirror and attached it to the wall, and made a lamp out of plaster lathe.

I did violate my own rule about not adding anything new by accepting the gift of a new water heater from my landlord and installing a shower. That was the extent of my conveniences; the rest of my needs were met in an outhouse—even in the dead of winter. I painted a flag on the door ('60s style) and suspended my stereo by a chain from the ceiling (otherwise the records would skip because the floor was so shaky). In the cold of winter I shivered beneath a pile of used blankets and quilts. On the coldest nights I slept on the floor in a sleeping bag in front of the coal oil heater.

In the summer I flung open all the doors and windows to let in any passing breath of air. I soon learned the lesson that window screens do not keep flies out—they keep them in. You never see flies sitting on the outside of a screen trying to get in. So I threw away the screens and waved at the bugs who flew through on their way to the barnyard, the smell of which wafted through my dwelling place on the early morning breezes. I measured my movements so as not to surprise the bees who also viewed the absence of screens as an invitation to take a shortcut to the fields of clover, which would later become the winter supply of cow food.

I was often honored by visits from various dogs, cats, and chickens who came to gawk curiously at me, the new farm animal. Sometimes they would come to visit me at night. I would wake in the morning to find them there—a dog I didn't recognize curled up beside me, a chicken perched on the window sill. Oh, the joy of waking surrounded by that impromptu gathering of farm animals. All of us humming along with the chorus of birds and bees and the percussion of mice scratching in the wall. The cows would add their mournful song, stretching their necks as they sang and struggling to prove once and for all that the grass on the other side is really greener.

My landlord and friend John had a daughter who one day brought home a puppy from school. It was the ugliest pup I had ever seen. It was not only ugly, it was clumsy and dumb. It grew up to be the biggest ugly dog imaginable: big, ugly, clumsy, *and* dumb. Proving the old adage that even dumb animals can find someone to love them, one day the dog came home pregnant and then gave birth to a dozen of the ugliest puppies you can imagine—ugly, clumsy, and dumb. I could sympathize with John's predicament; he was on the verge of an epidemic of ugly dogs. There was no hope of ever giving them away, so no one tried.

Then, one by one, the pups began to die. John's daughter was sad, but I knew that secretly John was quite relieved. The scourge of ugly dogs might pass. Then there were only two pups left: ugly, clumsy, dumb, and *sick*. John went out of town on business for a few days. As soon as he was gone, I took the two sick pups to the vet. They had been born with some sort of parasite, which accounted for the death of the others, but a shot and some nutrition put them right back on track again. Those two pups grew up to be every bit as big, ugly, and dumb as their mother.

I never confessed to John what I had done. I wonder if he guessed. He moved from the farm a few years later. In his letter he said it was because of another job offer, but I have always suspected that it was because the farm had been overrun by big, ugly, dumb dogs. I learned a sense of the sacredness of life during my Walden experience that has never left me.

Naturally, I chose for a wife a woman who takes lizards and mice gently out of the cat's mouth and carries them in the middle of the night to the safety of the canyon behind our house. And the little spiders that seem to congregate in bath tubs, she captures them for release outside in the rose bushes. Sometimes I tease her about it, but inwardly I admire and love her for her gentleness with all life.

I had a dog while I lived at John's farm, a little terrier. She was small, bright, and very quick (she proved that by challenging the bulls in the pens and just escaping with her life over and over again). But there were other dangers to face as well, there was the road out front where the cars came by much faster than the bulls in the pen and there were the hungry coyotes in the back forty. The question was whether to pen the little dog for her own safety or to let her run. John and I discussed the issue at length. I remember his words: "There is some risk in all of life." I believe that. I also believe that risk is a necessary ingredient for life to be life.

So the dog ran free and was always there to greet me when I returned home from road trips. One day she wasn't there to greet me and I never knew why, but I didn't second-guess my decision. It's better to live one's life with joy and freedom and have it ended early by a speeding car or a wild animal than to endure a long, safe nonlife in a pen.

That was my two years on the farm in Ohio. I never realized how eccentric the whole thing appeared until I started dating a young woman from the community. One night we went to her old alma mater for a basketball game. As we walked into the gymnasium, I had the immediate feeling that all eyes were on me. Then I heard someone say, "Isn't that the hippy who lives in the barn?" It was the first time it had occurred to me that that was indeed who I was. It was a period in my life I will never forget and never repeat. I can now say with Thoreau, "At present I am a sojourner in civilized life again."

I now live in a tract house in a walled housing development in suburbia. I like it here, too. How can the same person feel at home here and in the barn attic? I don't know; it's a mystery. Perhaps it's possible because I'm not a one-dimensional person. No one is. It's all part of the wondrous, walking contradiction that is me.

6

The Two-Headed Monster

Negative terms can be very useful; they help define the parameters of things. By saying what a thing is not, we can begin to circumscribe its general character before beginning the process of a more detailed understanding of what it is. So, in a way, negative values can be very positive.

It is said that Thomas Edison conducted 50,000 experiments while trying to invent a storage battery. One of his assistants complained about the lack of results, to which Edison supposedly replied, "Results? Why man, we have gotten lots of results. We know 50,000 things that won't work."

Most of the Ten Commandments are in negative terms. There are not as many "Thou shalts" as there are "Thou shalt nots." The signs along the highway tell the same story. There are as many telling you what not to do as there are those telling you what to do: Do Not Enter, No Parking, etc. Paul's eloquent description of love in 1 Corinthians 13 concerns itself mostly with what love is not, so you can tell if you don't have it.

Perhaps by circumscribing the indefinable in negative terms we can catch a glimpse of what it is by contrast. That, indeed, can be the best way to understand some things.

During my last year in seminary, I volunteered a couple of hours a week at an after-school, drop-in center for ghetto kids on the west side of Dayton, Ohio. It was quite an experience for this middle-class, white, small-town boy from Kansas who assumed his traditional values were more or less universal. Things like honesty and cleanliness, saluting the flag, being quiet in church, honoring your father and mother were behaviors I assumed everyone was taught around the world.

I discovered that many of these kids in West Dayton did not embrace those values I considered normative, particularly where parents were concerned. Many of them didn't know who their fathers were, and, if they did, they didn't consider them with much respect or love. Some fathers were abusive to their wives and terrifying to the children. On the week before Mother's Day we devised a crafts project; we would make Mother's Day cards. We got construction paper, crayons, and paste and instructed the kids to draw a picture on the inside of the card of the gift they would like to give to their mother if they could get them anything they wanted. One kid drew a picture of a gun. When, with some surprise, I asked why, he answered, "So she can shoot my old man when he comes home drunk."

This experience raised for me the issue of using the image of the father for God. I had always been so pleased with the image because it seemed to me to picture so well the nature of the relationship between humans and God. But now I wasn't so sure. How could these kids be taught that God was like a loving father when their own fathers were either absent or violent? I pressed the issue with some of the kids and discovered that, yes, they could relate to the image of a loving father. They understood the concept through their experience of the negative. They knew what one wasn't. They knew what they were missing. The vision of a loving father was etched clearly in their minds out of contrast with a life of negative experience.

There was a television Christmas drama several years ago that I have never forgotten. There is so little substantive programing on television that when a truly creative piece comes along it has a way of sticking in the memory. The story was about a cowboy who had planned for a whole year to go to the Christmas dance in town. You see, he had met a girl there the year before. He had saved his money and bought a bolt of cloth and a box of candy for her. The night finally came, he put on his new red shirt, gathered up his gifts, and headed for town.

On the way he passed a woman chopping wood. He asked her why her husband wasn't doing that hard work, and she told him that her husband was sick and she had to care for him and their two young children. So the cowboy got off his horse, chopped a load of wood for the woman and carried it into the house. Inside the house, he noticed that there wasn't a Christmas tree. He asked, "Where is your Christmas tree? You've gotta have a Christmas tree!" She, a little indignant, shot back, "I suppose when you were a little boy you always had a Christmas tree?" "No, I never did," he said softly, "that's how I know how important it is."

We can know the worth of things by not having them. We can know the dimension of things by circumscribing them with what they are not. We can enhance the possibility of bringing good things to our lives by eliminating their opposites. We can enrich life by avoiding the things that are deadly. There is no point in trying to grow a lovely garden if we water it with battery acid. We can't hope to have a healthy, beautiful body if we feed it DDT.

The two-headed monster of jealousy and anger is like acid and poison to the health and well-being of our spirits. It's important to focus on the positive. To reinvoke the highway metaphor, if we persist in driving on the wrong side of the road at night with our lights off, all the positive driving habits in the world are not going to help us. My goal in discussing these negative influences is that by doing so, our awareness of their positive counterparts in our lives will be heightened and that the beauty of the positives will become a reality for us by eliminating the negatives.

Let me say this in very specific terms: under no circumstances should we let the two-headed monster of jealousy and anger gain a foothold in our lives! Now I know that there are other negative forces out there ready to lay waste to our spiritual well-being—in fact, I will refer to some of them in following chapters—but these two are so insidious and treacherous as to call for special consideration. My experience with them and the experiences shared with me in counseling sessions convince me that jealousy and anger are the major assassins of the spirit at large today. The special insidiousness of their characters is that they slide into our behavior patterns so easily; they come disguised as charm and righteous indignation. At first they seem comfortable, compatible houseguests for the spirit. They are con artists, however, these twin monsters of jealousy and anger.

Anger is at first exhilarating and exciting. There is a scene in the movie *Inside Moves* where one friend betrayed by another goes to have it out. He unloads his righteous anger with amazing eloquence. When the object of his rage tries to interrupt to explain, he says, "Don't stop me. I'm mad and I feel good. I'm big, even bigger than you." Quite a statement, considering that his friend was a professional basketball player. Anger can do that for you; it can make your blood pump and make you a couple feet taller before it turns on you.

Jealousy

Jealousy is tricky and cruel in that it often enters our spirits through the doorway of love; indeed, it is often mistaken for love itself. When you truly love someone, you pay a great deal of attention to that person; you want to be with her as much as possible; you want her to want to be with you. If the object of your affection should drop out of sight each day for an hour or so, the jealousy monster raises its ugly head and whispers that your love is doing something she doesn't want you to know about or even involve yourself with.

We need to be reminded regularly that a necessary component of love is trust. When jealousy removes that trust, love turns to possessiveness. You can see it in its earliest and purest form on high-school campuses. There they are, the star of the football team and the head cheerleader walking hand in hand across campus. What could be a more lovely picture? They love each other. Or do they? Could it be that both of them are not so much focused on the other person but on the crowd of peers on the school grounds. Look again. Is their handholding an act of affectionate touching or possession? Is the statement behind that lovely symbolic act "Look who I love" or "Look what I own! I have control of the hottest chick [or the biggest hunk] on campus"? Let that hunk or chick show attention to another attractive person and then see if love/trust gets expressed. Is it love or ownership? Is it concern for the other person's spiritual growth and well-being (which is how Scott Peck defines love) or is it concern for one's image and property that is at stake?

The constant companion of love must be trust. When young couples ask me how they can know if they are truly in love, I offer that word as a test. "Do you trust each other implicitly?" Trust is a good love indicator. People who really love don't question the fidelity of their lovers. That's why we say that love is blind: a true lover is always the last to know or believe that his or her lover is unfaithful. When a meeting time comes and goes and an hour passes, the trusting person begins to construct mental images of traffic accidents or other emergencies but never entertains the monstrous assumption that he or she is being hidden from or avoided. Love trusts; jealousy suspects. Jealousy imprisons; love sets free.

The phrase "Free Love" was quite popular in the 1960s and appeared on lots of buttons and bumper stickers. Unfortunately, what was implied by that slogan had little to do with either love or freedom. A more precise phrase might have been "Unrestrained Sexuality." The phrase "Free Love" strikes me as interesting because it is redundant. Love is, by definition, always free. It's a lovely paradox that the force that drives you to want to spend all of your time with and pay all of your attention to another person, to know him or her inside and out, will be the same force that makes you want the best of everything for that person, even if what is best for her or him isn't you!

In the marriage ceremony, the word *cherish* appears more than once. I tell couples in premarital counseling that to cherish means to care about another person's well-being as much as you care about your own. The Bible says it another way, "and the two shall become one" (Matt. 19:5). When two people are bound in love, what affects one of them affects both of them, almost as if they were one organism. They care about each other's well-being as much as their own because it is their own. Where can the concept of jealousy possibly fit in that scenario? Love trusts. It sets free. Jealousy kills all of that before it has a chance to live and bloom.

In Paul's description of love, to which I referred earlier, he uses the word *jealous* to circumscribe and define what love is not: "Love is not jealous or boastful; it is not arrogant or rude. Love does not insist on its own way; it is not irritable or resentful; it does not rejoice at wrong" (1 Cor. 13:4–6). That last statement gets at one of the ugliest manifestations of jealousy imaginable: to rejoice at wrong. Jealous people love it when bad things happen to other people. Love grieves when bad things happen to other people, even if they are people you don't necessarily like or people who are in competition with you. It is said that Abraham Lincoln refused to celebrate victory in the American Civil War because he knew that one man's victory was another's defeat and that the defeated, suffering South was also America.

When the news first broke about the nuclear power plant disaster at Chernobyl, I was at a church for a meeting and we were discussing the event briefly before the meeting started. One man came in late in the conversation and hadn't heard the news. At that time, it was thought that perhaps thousands had died. He eagerly chimed in, "Where was that?" "In the Soviet Union," I said. "Oh," he smiled, "then that's OK." The poor man didn't know much about Christianity or even humanity and certainly nothing about love. Love wishes the best for people, even people we might consider our enemies.

Suppose two of you are up for a promotion, or a part in the school play, or an elected office. Can you rejoice with your victorious opponent if you don't like her or him, if you are better qualified than she or he? If so, then you know something about real love. The monster of jealousy has been slain in you, and the spirit in you can grow to glorious health and beauty.

Anger

Now let me speak of jealousy's surviving twin, anger. It sucks the spirit dry, colors your perceptions of the world, clouds your analysis of other people's behavior, and contaminates your whole being from the inside out.

In *Wishful Thinking*, Frederick Buechner wrote, "Of the Seven Deadly Sins, anger is possibly the most fun. To lick your wounds, to smack your lips over grievances long past, to roll over your tongue the prospect of bitter confrontations still to come, to savor to the last toothsome morsel both the pain you are given and the pain you are giving back—in many ways it is a feast fit for a king. The chief drawback is that what you are wolfing down is yourself. The skeleton at the feast is you."

Earlier I stated that anger is exhilarating and energizing at first. Some people use it to stimulate life. Let me give you an example from my experience.

I once lived next door to a grouch. I never saw her because she was a short grouch, and everyone in California has a high fence in their backyard. But I could hear her out there grouching at the dog, at the geraniums, at life in general. One day she caught me, saw in hand, preparing to cut a branch off of what she thought was her tree. I thought it was my tree. It was pretty close to the line since the fence was attached to it. Anyhow, I thought I at least had the right to trim the branches that hung over my garage and plugged my drains with leaves. She assured me that I was wrong. There she was, almost ninety pounds of wrinkled-up old flesh, flailing her arms and shouting obscenities at me up there in "her" tree. I slinked down the tree and limped into my house, bruised by—and amazed at—the power of this little grouch I had encountered.

I read somewhere that the factor that most determines how well we like where we live is how well we get along with our neighbors. I think that's correct. So I took on my grouchy neighbor as a project. I wasn't going to live next door to a grouch, and I wasn't going to move. That left one option: I had to win her over. At Christmastime my church is decorated with hundreds of poinsettias and some are always left there. I picked the biggest one I could find (that sucker was a tree) and placed it on her front porch with a note that read "Have a lovely Christmas season. Your neighbor, Bob." The next day the doorbell rang and there she was, the grouch, standing on my porch holding a jar of homemade applesauce. The ploy had worked; she had taken the bait. My gesture of reconciliation had prompted her to respond in kind. For the rest of the years I lived there, my refrigerator never knew a shortage of applesauce.

So there we were, talking like real neighbors on my front porch. For the better part of an hour she told me the story of her life, and a sad tale it was. She told me about everyone who had used, abused, and done her wrong. Especially, she told me about her alcoholic husband with whom she had suffered for thirty years until he finally had the decency to die. As she talked, her face screwed up into a frown and got red, her fists clenched until her knuckles turned white, and her voice became bitter between her gritted teeth. Then it occurred to me—everything she was describing had happened more than twenty years ago. She had lived with that anger so long that she had no recollection of the good times nor any expectation of warmth forthcoming from anyone. Her world-view was colored by anger, and she herself was defined by it and driven by it. If there is such a thing as demon possession, this was like it; she was possessed by her anger. If only she could have heard and internalized the words of Paul the Apostle who said to the people at Ephesus, "Be angry, but do not sin." Then in the next line he told them how that is done. "Don't let the sun go down on your anger."

Anger itself is not the problem. As a matter of fact a little anger is a good motivator. Lots of constructive change has come from it as well as lots of stimulating debate and creative solutions. The problem is not the anger. It's what you do with it. Bottled-up anger soon turns to vinegar and eventually to gall. It becomes a poison that eats away at you from the inside. So don't be a bottle—be a funnel. Let the anger run through and exhilarate you, but make sure it has all drained out by nightfall. The next day it won't be so easy to deal with; it will have started to change already and it will begin to change you.

In *Fully Human, Fully Alive,* John Powell has said, "Obnoxious qualities in myself and in others are really cries of pain and appeals for help." People who seem to be angry at everyone and everything are usually only angry with themselves. They have not turned out like they had hoped. Life played a dirty trick on them. They are neither smart, successful, nor beautiful, so they blame everyone else and life itself for dealing them a rotten hand. Consider this possibility: if everything goes wrong all the time, maybe it's not everything at all, maybe it's you. Instead of looking around for some convenient place to hang the blame for your life, look inward for the ugliness that has cast its shadow over everything else.

I once told a woman, "You don't have an inferiority complex, you really are inferior." She didn't think that was funny. Angry people can't find the humor in things, especially themselves. It has already begun to change them from the inside out, and they are quickly becoming all those things they hate. They are a walking self-fulfilled prophecy being molded into the image of the anger that dwells within. Don't let the sun go down on your anger. Find a way to vent it, release it, or channel it before it eats you alive. It is the acid of the spirit. Beware.

"Be angry but do not sin; do not let the sun go down on your anger, and give no opportunity to the devil. . . . Let all bitterness and wrath and anger and clamor and slander be put away from you, with all malice" (Eph. 4:26–27, 31). You see, Paul understood the power of negative terms, except his monster had many more heads than mine. From time to time people tell me that they don't read the Bible because they don't understand it. I tell them to read until they find something they do understand. These two verses from Paul are perfectly clear, they circumscribe in negative terms what the Christian life ought to look like. One could spend a lifetime trying to accomplish the ideal inherent in these two verses and still come up short, but what a lovely journey it would be.

Paul also knew the value of positive terms. I offer his next two verses as homework for us all for the rest of our lives:

> Be kind to one another, tenderhearted, forgiving one an-
> other, as God in Christ forgave you. Therefore be imitators
> of God, as beloved children.
>
> *Eph. 4:32–5:1*

- Take stock of yourself: Are your love relationships characterized by trust or suspicion? Do you cling or set free? Does your anger pass quickly and leave you energized or linger to devour you?

- Jealousy and anger—get rid of them. When they move into your spirit, kick them out. Prayer helps. It's hard to be angry with someone at the same time you are asking God to bless him or her. It's hard to remain jealous when you are in the presence of a loving God asking to be made more like His Son.

7

Target Fixation

A few years ago I decided to take some hang gliding lessons. It happened one day when I was on a hike and walking along a windy ridge. I held out my arms to embrace the wind, and, leaning into it, I wanted more than anything just to spring off the edge and trust the friendly wind to hold me up as it did the hawk that soared just beyond my land-bound mortal reach. So I took my first lesson. After the preliminaries about safety and how to put the device together, I dragged my kite to the top of a round hill and felt that same inviting wind in my face. The instructor below placed a huge red canvas in the middle of the grassy landing area. The valley must have been about twice the size of a football field. He said that the canvas was the target. I laughed at that. A field that big would be hard to miss whether we had the red canvas to shoot for or not.

That's when I was introduced to the term "target fixation." He said that once we were in flight we would see a big rock just beyond the field or an oak tree by the stream, and we would fly right into it. He said, "You tend to fly toward what you look at." The red canvas provided a target, something to fixate on, and most of the class landed right on it.

There is an old proverb that says, "If we don't change our direction we are likely to end up where we are headed." This is as good a place as any to introduce the intensely religious word, *repentance*. To repent is to make a "U" turn. We repent when we realize that the direction in which we are heading is not getting us to where we want to be, so we turn around and start in the other direction. It doesn't mean instant success, holiness, or satisfaction. The road back is just as far as it was coming the other way.

Yogi Berra, my favorite baseball philosopher, is credited with saying, "We may be lost, but we're making good time." Making good progress in the wrong direction is not good planning.

Since I believe it is true that we tend to travel toward what we fixate on, then perhaps we should carefully choose those targets and, if necessary, repent, lest we end up where we are headed.

World-view

Much has been written about thinking positively. Far be it from me to try to match the likes of Norman Vincent Peale, Robert Schuller, and Dale Carnegie. I recommend that you pull those books off the shelf and read them again. I simply remind you here that there is a certain what-you-see-is-what-you-get-ness about life. How you view the world is how the world views you and determines what the world tends to dish out. Some people get up in the morning and say, "This is going to be a lousy day." They go through the day saying, "This is going to be a lousy day." Then they go to bed at night saying, "See there, I was right." Their only satisfaction in life is always being right. The last beatitude that Jesus left off the list is this one, "Blessed are they who expect nothing, for they shall not be disappointed." Modern translation—"What you see *is* what you get." If you don't see anything, you don't get anything.

One of my favorite Joni Mitchell songs is "Chelsea Morning."

> Woke up it was a Chelsea morning
> and the first thing that I knew
> there was milk and toast and honey
> and a bowl of oranges too.
> And the light poured in like butterscotch
> and stuck to all my senses.

> Won't you stay, we'll put on the day
> and we'll talk in present tenses.

"And the light poured in like butterscotch." What a marvelous image! I grew up in a home in which my mother, first thing in the morning, would close the curtains on the east side of the house and open the curtains on the west side of the house. Then about mid-afternoon, she would open the curtains on the east side of the house and close the curtains on the west side. Why? Because the light poured in like bleach and faded the carpet. Are you a person for whom the light pours in like butterscotch or bleach? It has to do with your world-view. Does the light of a new day signal the beginning of a new adventure, or does it represent a threat to your investment? Is your world a flower garden or a minefield? What you see is what you get.

That the world keeps turning and changing is a fact of life. It is the nature of life to be unpredictable and filled with surprises. Does that thought make you smile or frown? Some older people become angry grouches because they lock themselves up and insist that the world outside remain unchanged. They keep their little world the same: same furniture, same unfaded carpet, same way of thinking. Then they look out the window and see that the world has moved on without them and feel betrayed. But that's the nature of the world and that's the fun of it. The primary definition of the terms *liberal* and *conservative* have to do with precisely that, how one deals with the fact of change. The conservative digs in his heels and resists change; "It was that way when I was a kid and I want it that way now." Witness a conservative president restoring old World War II battleships. "If it worked for Harry Truman, it will work for me." Someone said that a conservative is one who believes that nothing should be done for the first time. The liberal, on the other hand, embraces change and indeed encourages it; "If it worked once, that is good enough reason not to do it again." Professor John Cobb said in a speech, "Why do we argue over whether communism or capitalism is the best economic system? One is a product of the eighteenth century and the other of the nineteenth. We should be bright enough in this century to come up with our own." That's a liberal point of view. In order to have a positive world-view one must see change not only as inevitable, but as positive. Every new door opens on a roomful of opportunity. Life has a way of fulfilling everyone's expectations. Blessed are they who expect good things and new adventures, for they shall not be disappointed. Life is change. You're moving. Be sure you are moving in the direction you want to go. Pick a worthy target.

There is a story about a man who moved from a city in the East to a city in the West. On his first visit to the new town he saw an old man walking down the street. He stopped the old man and asked, "How long have you lived in this town?" The old man replied "I've lived here all my life." The visitor was sure now that he had the right candidate for his next question. "Tell me," he said, "what kind of people will I find in this town?" The old man, being very wise, answered the question with another question. "What kind of people did you find in the town you came from?" "They were really fine people," the visitor replied. The old man said, "That's the kind of people you'll find here." Life is a self-fulfilling prophecy.

You have a choice of how you will perceive the world around you, and you tend to get what you expect, you tend to end up where you are headed. There is probably no such thing as true objectivity anyhow, so why not interpret things in your favor? David the shepherd boy had a choice. There he was confronted by the giant Goliath with his weapons, his armor, and his bulging biceps. David might have said, "Look how big he is, how can I win?" But instead he said, "Look how big he is, how can I miss!"

There is an old joke about twin boys, an optimist and a pessimist. The mother was worried about their drastically different personalities, so she took them to a child psychologist. The psychologist took the pessimist and put him in a room filled with beautiful toys. Everything was colorful and mechanical. Everything Mattel ever dreamed of was in there, and the batteries were included. He placed the optimist in a room, waist deep in manure. An hour later, he came by to check on each boy's progress. The pessimist in the toy room was unhappy. The toys were all broken and the batteries were run down. So he peeked in the window at the optimist, waist deep in manure. He had a big smile on his face—he was digging—and he said, "There has to be a pony in here somewhere."

Why not look positively on what life dishes out; it's your choice. "Two men looked through prison bars, one saw mud the other saw stars." It's not the circumstances of our lives that are all that different; it's our world-view. It's how we interpret those events that makes them tragedy or opportunity. There is this phrase in Paul's marvelous love poem in the thirteenth chapter of 1 Corinthians: "Love believes all things." I read an interpretation of that phrase that went like this: love puts the best possible face on other people's behavior. If you have several choices in understanding why people do the things they do, pick the kindest one. Love believes the best about other people.

Picture yourself driving down the freeway, doing 65 in a 55-mile-per-hour zone like everyone else, when some character in a silver gray 300ZX comes out of nowhere, across four lanes of traffic, and down the off ramp. You are furious! You are furious for a number of reasons: he is speeding more than you are, he didn't so much as glance back to see the hand gesture you offered him, he risked a collision that could have involved you, and he has a nicer car than you. So you immediately conclude that he is a lowlife jerk without consideration for God or humankind, and he probably is a litterbug as well and beats his children. All that you ascertain by observing some small moment of his behavior. Why would you do that? The incident is past; the man is gone. Why would you choose to let it have a negative impact on your whole day? You look at your speedometer and notice you have sped up to 70. In fact, you see, yours is the only day it will mess up. The other driver doesn't even know you exist, much less how you feel about him. Since all the effect is on you and the facts are at best sketchy, why not interpret the event in a kinder way? Maybe he has one of those car phones and the hospital just called to tell him that his wife has delivered their first child. That might even be enough to make you speed and go across four lanes of traffic. Well, actually, it was only three lanes if you don't count the one he was already in. Or, this is my favorite reading of that situation. He just heard his lottery ticket number read on the radio, and he's a member of my church, and he's a tither! Why not? If the definition of love is to put a kind face on other's people's behavior, then to love life is to put the best interpretation on what life hands you. This will take some practice. You will have to reject a lot of first impulses. Practice the technique and feel your spirit soar.

> Woke up it was a Chelsea morning
> and the first thing that I saw,
> Was the sun through yellow curtains
> and a rainbow on my wall.
> Red, blue, and green to welcome you,
> crimson crystal beads to beckon.
> Won't you stay, we'll put on the day
> there's a sun shower every second.

Take charge of the direction you will fly. You chose how you interpret the world around you and the events of your life. You chose your world-view and your self-image. But remember, there is a sense of self-fulfilling prophecy in it all. Your choices become targets that determine whether you ultimately land softly in the big grassy field or if you crack up somewhere on the ragged edge of life.

How you think of the world and of other people is finally an expression of how you feel about yourself. People who are always finding fault with another's behavior probably spot those behaviors because they are so much like their own. Most behavior that expresses itself as anger toward others is really self-loathing. In other words, it's impossible to have high goals and worthy targets unless you have a good self-image. John Powell notes, "A good self-image is the most valuable psychological possession of a human being."

I meet lots of people who don't set lofty goals because they don't consider themselves worthy of achieving them. They seem to sabotage their own flight. They choose the rocks as a target, and they crash right into them.

A common closing greeting in our society is "Be good to yourself." That should be the easiest of all advice to follow; after all, our selves are all we have. If we aren't good to us, who will be? We need to ask ourselves the following questions: Am I really good to me? Do I treat myself like a priceless gift? If someone else treated me like I treat me, would I call that good? Do I eat the most nutritious foods? Do I exercise? Do I get plenty of relaxation and sleep? Do I take time for personal renewal? If we aren't doing any of these for ourselves, perhaps we should take a long look at the targets we have chosen. Choosing worthy goals is the outcome of being good to ourselves, which is the natural outcome of liking ourselves.

Self-esteem expresses itself in a variety of ways. Here, though, I want to pick up just two words; words that may seem like strange bedfellows but are the kind of words that are essential if one is to feel good about oneself and aspire to high goals. The words are *fun* and *discipline*.

Fun

Do you ever do anything just because it's fun? Yes, fun! Fun is one of those words that fall into a secondary category of importance when we list our priorities. We tend to think that it's okay to have fun if it's a fringe benefit of a more worthwhile endeavor. Most of us can't imagine setting out just for the purpose of fun; it seems so frivolous, so juvenile, so wasteful. Even activities that were once fun, like sports events, are no longer fun. They are now desperately serious. Instead of being a respite from tension, they contribute to it. So the question remains. Do you ever do anything just for the fun of it? You deserve some fun!

I have a list that I use in counseling couples before marriage. It's a list of what I call keys to a successful marriage. There on that list of lofty concepts like commitment, values, and communication is the word *fun*. Couples are surprised to see it there. I am quick to defend its rightful place. Fun will sustain a good marriage as well as loyalty and respect. Life is too short, I tell them, to spend it with someone who is no fun. So one of the questions I ask them to reflect on is whether they have fun together. You might be surprised at the hesitancy in couples as they glance uneasily at one another trying to answer that question honestly. If I ask, "Do you love him/her?" the answer is a quick and definite affirmative, but if I ask, "Is he/she fun?" that's a harder question to answer.

Celebration is one of those words at home with religion and the rest of society as well. It's hard to imagine a celebration devoid of fun; indeed a celebration that is no fun is a dismal failure. We call the worship services at my church "Worship celebrations." When I plan what ingredients go into that worship service, I always make sure that that includes an element of fun. Fun does not negate reverence, but its absence negates celebration.

The nature of fun, however, has changed because of too much processing and packaging. Instead of "we the people" defining fun, it's defined for us by those who market it. Just like a frozen dinner, it may look like food, but it bears no real resemblance to those fresh vegetables you might pick out of your own garden. So I recommend that people with healthy spirits not only make fun a priority but go for natural, homegrown fun, not the processed commercial kind. Homemade fun is the real stuff; the packaged, processed stuff is a pale imitation. Unfortunately, a whole generation of people has been raised on the processed stuff, and they have come to like it better.

I read at Christmastime last year about a subtle shift in emphasis among Christmas tree merchants. Where once imitation trees were made to look like real trees, now Christmas tree growers are trying to make live trees look more like the imitation ones. The trunk must be perfectly straight. The needles cannot fall off. We have grown so accustomed to the imitation that the real cannot compete. So imitation, processed, and packaged fun is the order of the day for the latest generation. No wonder brides and grooms can't answer whether their prospective spouse is fun. They aren't supposed to be fun. Disneyland is supposed to be fun. Where else can you rocket to Mars and slide down the Matterhorn on the same day; see bears sing and Michael Jackson dance and ghosts fly around a haunted ballroom? Where else can you drop that much cash that fast and stand in line until your legs drop off all in the name of fun?

Not long ago I was in Orlando for a few days and went to have a look at the East Coast version of Disneyland. Since I was alone, I had ample opportunity to engage in one of my favorite pastimes, people watching. I looked for signs and symbols of people having fun. I saw few smiles or expressions of joy or anticipation. Instead I saw crowding and pushing and that harried look that comes from trying to cover every attraction in a single day. There were tired kids and grouchy parents, reluctant participants in an American ritual called having fun. Once at Disneyland (the one in California), I observed a mother spanking her child and scolding him, saying, "We paid a lot of money for this and you're going to enjoy it!"

The healthy, beautiful spirit has to reclaim fun. Its definition and creation have to belong to us, not to profit-making corporations. We have to grab it away from the technology that is robbing fun of its true essence.

For several years I directed a church summer camp for high-school-aged youth. One of the rules that I vigorously enforced was the one banning radios, tapedecks, or any other electronic, music-producing device. There was tremendous resistance to my rule. If the camp operation had been a democracy, I could never have pulled it off. But it was a benevolent dictatorship, with me as the benevolent dictator. So they would come with their boom boxes blasting. The most insidious ones are those that plug directly into the ears providing perfect isolation from the outside world. Those devices precluded sharing on any level, so I would confiscate all of them and lock them in the trunk of my car. The grumbling would escalate over the next couple of days as the withdrawal pains began to intensify. No prerecorded music for two days can make you crazy. Sometimes there was talk of mass rebellion, even mutiny. I stationed a guard at the trunk of my car.

On the third day, a miracle would happen. Someone would get out an old guitar or peck out a tune on a piano. Little groups would form and begin to create their own homemade music. It's one of life's ironies, how homemade music creates community while processed music creates isolation. There would be joy and glad expressions on faces, the like of which I have seldom seen at Disneyland. They were experiencing, perhaps for the first time, the wonder of homemade fun. It wasn't high class or high quality music, but it was theirs, a group effort, a group process, born among giggles, shrieks, harmonic errors, and the surprise of accomplishment.

When Jesus and His band traveled around the hills of Galilee and up and down the Jordan River Valley, they did so on foot. There were no devices to entertain them on their way from Jericho up to Jerusalem. I wonder what they did as they walked together or sat around the campfire at night. Maybe someone got out an old stringed instrument and they sang some songs together, perhaps some of the songs of His ancestor David. Maybe the disciples knew Jesus so well and came to love Him so deeply in such a short period of time because He not only taught them and challenged them, but He sang with them, and together they had fun.

My most profound experience of homemade music came when I attended a spring bluegrass festival in Mountain View, Arkansas. By the time I discovered this annual event, technology was already creeping in, threatening to spoil its purity. But the festival was putting up some pretty strong resistance. Other threats, however, were coming from those who love to categorize and organize. They built a stage in front of the courthouse and, yes, they even installed a row of microphones. Thankfully, no one of significance would stand on stage, use the microphones, or otherwise conform to a performance schedule. All the good pickers were in impromptu gatherings around behind the courthouse, facing each other and smiling. Surrounding them was a larger circle of listeners. They didn't play for the audience, they played for the fun of it. Their picking was a celebration for themselves. Young mandolin players and old fiddlers, some good, some not so good, were all welcome at this homemade music festival.

Driving back to my motel, I saw a bunch of cars parked along the blacktop for no apparent reason. I stopped to investigate. There was a path leading from the road down a steep slope through the pine trees. I followed it in the darkness for about a half mile until I began to hear music. There, at the end of the path, was a crowd of people gathered in front of a log cabin (a *real* log cabin, not the kind you see at amusement parks). There was a bearded man, wearing bib overalls, sitting on the porch playing a fiddle. His wife came out and picked some banjo for a while, too, then she went back in the house to go to bed. She had to get up early in the morning to do her chores.

I stayed. I smiled. I clapped my hands. I even enjoyed the people who were there with me. They were not quite strangers; we were bound together by the mutual discovery of a treasure. I remember that experience vividly though many years have passed. It was fun!

I have resisted the urge to go back to Mountain View since then because I fear that by now the organizers may have won. All the performances may be on stage according to a printed schedule, and the path to the log cabin probably has lights and a hand rail and an admission fee.

My parents and their friends used to have card parties. No money was involved, just goofy prizes for the winners and the losers. As a child, I didn't understand how their card game was played. All I knew was that they traded tables and they laughed a lot. Then we would make some homemade ice cream. (It bore no resemblance at all to that cold substance by the same name in the supermarkets.) If it was winter, we would chop the ice out of the cow pond, and all of us kids took turns turning the crank on the freezer. If it was spring, we used homegrown strawberries for a topping. We would play hide-and-seek and capture-the-flag until we were exhausted. Then we would crawl into the backseat of the Ford for the ride home and drift off to sleep to the hum of Dad's flathead V-8.

It was an experience that couldn't be purchased at any price. It was priceless and it was free. It was fun. It was homemade. I would dare say that my parents also never felt so alive as during those card-playing, ice-cream-making celebrations of life.

Healthy spirits must choose their targets wisely. Technology that advertises itself as fun is like the tree and the rock on the edge of the landing field. Unless we find a worthy target, we will probably fly straight into the ragged fringe of life. People with good self-images will define their own terms, thank you, and not be pushed around by image makers, market managers, and those who institutionalize fun.

The question is begged; who tells you what is fun? (Probably the same sources that tell you what is important.) For example, do you ever do anything just because you are good at it? It may not be of economic worth or importance to anyone else, but you do it just for the satisfaction of doing something you're good at. Can you think of something you're good at separate from its marketability? It may have been years since you thought about it.

When you went to school, no one asked what you were good at. They stuck you in math, science, English, and history, all the things you would need to get you through life. When you chose a career, you didn't necessarily choose what you were good at, but rather something in a field in which "they" were hiring and something you could make a good living doing. Most people spend their lives at jobs they hate in order to make enough money to do what they want in their free time. But even when you chose a hobby you probably picked something that your friends thought was cool and was commensurate with your social status. Princes play polo; they don't go bowling; but what if you're a member of the royal family and a scratch bowler or a polo-loving pauper? What are you really good at? You may need to think about that for a moment.

A phrase emerged in the turbulent '60s that the dropout generation both understood and put into practice: "Do your own thing." It meant that what you do is valuable simply because it's an expression of yourself, separate from its salability or social significance. So a person would be seen sitting on the front porch, staring off into the cosmos. When someone would ask what he was doing, he would answer, "I'm doing my own thing." That was enough to validate the activity, or inactivity, as the case may be. It was a radical idea for people who were reared with the same pressure to accomplish and do important things as you and I.

There was an episode on "Hill Street Blues" about a cop who didn't want to be a cop. He didn't like guns and violence. The problem was that his father was a cop, and his father before him, and he had graduated at the top of his class at the police academy. Everyone agreed, he had to be a cop. In a touching conversation with Captain Furillo, who was at his compassionate best, the young cop confessed that what he really enjoyed doing was cabinetmaking. His eyes danced as he talked about the joy of stroking the wood, shaping it with his hands, and making it come alive. Then Furillo, almost like a priest blessing a devout parishioner, set him free with these words: "Go and be a cabinetmaker, and be a good cabinetmaker." It was as if that load accumulated over a lifetime had been lifted as he rose to begin a new life.

So now that you have had some time to think about it, what do you really like to do? Don't be embarrassed. Rosey Grier likes to do needlepoint. I know men who are good at delicate needlework or who write sensitive poetry and women who like to work on cars. Forget the role stereotypes and preconceived notions.

Identify the thing you do really well and do it. I'm not suggesting that you rush out and quit your job. I am suggesting that at least a small part of that to which you give your time, indeed, that for which you trade your life, ought to be something that is valuable simply because it is yours and doing it sets your spirit free.

Personally, I think it's best if your "thing" is something that offers immediate gratification, like building a birdhouse or growing a garden. You can see and measure the progress with each nail you drive or seed you plant. Then you can lean back on your hoe as often and for as long as you like and admire your work. I also think it's better if it's something that produces calluses, blisters, sweat, and even dirt under your fingernails. But it's your thing. It's God's gift to you and your gift to the world. Don't estimate its economic value at the current exchange rate. Don't compare it to what others are doing. Just do it, celebrate it, and offer it to the world.

This verse from a Joni Mitchell song reads like a confession:

> Me, I play for fortunes and those velvet curtain calls.
> I've got a black limousine
> and two gentlemen escorting me to the halls.
> And I'll play if you have the money
> or if you're a friend to me.
> But the one-man band by the quick lunchstand,
> He was playing real good for free.
>
> Nobody stopped to hear him
> Though he played so sweet and high.
> They knew he had never been on their TV
> So they passed his music by.
> I meant to go over and ask for a tune
> Maybe put on a harmony
> I heard his refrain as the signal changed
> He was playing real good for free.

Discipline

Since I have said so much in this chapter about focusing on oneself, one's goals (targets), fun, and self-interest, it seems good to discuss *discipline* in the next breath. To be self-aware and healthy is to be self-disciplined. Before you rush to the conclusion that I am now taking all the fun out of it, read on. Like fun, discipline doesn't mean what most people think.

In *The Road Less Traveled*, Scott Peck says:

> Discipline is the basic set of tools we require to solve life's problems. Without discipline we can solve nothing. With only some discipline we can solve only some problems. With total discipline we can solve all problems. . . .
>
> What makes life difficult is that the process of confronting and solving problems is a painful one. Problems, depending upon their nature, evoke in us frustration or a grief or sadness or loneliness or guilt or regret or anger or fear or anxiety or anguish or despair. These are uncomfortable feelings, often very uncomfortable, often as painful as any kind of physical pain, sometimes equaling the very worst kind of physical pain. Indeed, it is because of the pain that events or conflicts engender in us that we call them problems. And since life poses an endless series of problems, life is always difficult and is full of pain as well as joy. . . .
>
> Therefore let us inculcate in ourselves and in our children the means of achieving mental and spiritual health. By this I mean let us teach ourselves and our children the necessity for suffering and the value thereof, the need to face problems directly and to experience the pain involved. I have stated that discipline is the basic set of tools we require to solve life's problems. It will become clear that these tools are techniques of suffering, means by which we experience the pain of problems in such a way as to work them through and solve them successfully, learning and growing in the process. When we teach ourselves and our children discipline, we are teaching them and ourselves how to suffer and also how to grow.

These excerpts are from the first few pages of the book. I have to confess that when I read them I almost closed the book and put it on the shelf. Those two words are used over and over in the first chapter, *discipline* and *suffering*. Who wants to read about them, particularly when the writer advocates the notion that they're good for you and necessary tools for doing life successfully? I did read on, however, because Peck also slipped the word *joy* in there with them, and I couldn't resist the pull of that combination.

Of those two words—discipline and suffering—the most repugnant to me is the first. Suffering is at least a word filled with color and emotion. It conjures up images of bloody battles, dying alone on a sun-parched desert, or a plague-ravaged continent. When I think of suffering, I think of Job sitting on a pile of rubble that used to be his sprawling ranch-style home, scraping his scab-covered body with a piece of broken pottery, mourning the death of his wife and children. Of course, I also think of Jesus weeping over Jerusalem because the people would not be gathered in under the protective wings of God. I think of His agonizing prayer in the garden, His humiliation, rejection, and crucifixion. That's suffering! That last week of Jesus' life is correctly called Passion Week. Suffering is passion, is real, is filled with the stuff of life, and is the material of which heroism is made.

Discipline, in comparison, seems like such a bland word. It evokes images no more significant than that of cleaning up your room, not talking with your mouth full, not biting your fingernails, or sticking to a diet. Discipline seems to counteract spontaneity, and spontaneity is the source of some of life's richest and most creative moments. Discipline implies orderliness and structure, and, as I have said earlier, something in me resists those things. I prefer my life as a creative jumble. A little suffering I can deal with, but discipline . . . ?

Still I cannot escape the fact that within the Christian faith, or any religion for that matter, there are certain disciplines. A great many spiritual benefits can be gained by submitting oneself to those disciplines. In fact, irony of ironies, there is a certain liberating effect that follows, a sense of taking charge of one's own life, of being the captain of your own soul. That kind of discipline that sets one free is the self-imposed kind. It is to do something just because you said you would. If you do something for a reward, you have your reward. But if you do it out of self-discipline, the reward is spiritual growth.

One of the colleges I attended was operated by a conservative church denomination. On campus, things were run like most private schools, but there was a constituency out there that had to be pleased if the money was going to keep coming. So certain vestiges of that conservative constituency crept into campus life.

The registration materials included a pledge that I was to sign. It included, among other things, a promise not to attend any movies. I thought it was a silly rule, what with the movie capital of the world being just over the hill. We were supposed to be adults now, capable of making choices as to what was and wasn't good for us. In those days we used to love to point out that if we were old enough to fight and die in Vietnam, we should be old enough to vote, drink, and go to movies. Besides all that, it was a hypocritical rule. If movies were a no-no, why was there no prohibition against watching movies on television in the dorm?

The pledge, however, was part of the registration procedure, so I signed it and probably intended to keep it; at least until I discovered that very few of my classmates intended to observe the pledge, especially since there was a movie theater down the street with a $1 matinee special. That was the only form of entertainment this poor college kid could afford. That was that. I forgot about the pledge and went on with my life.

But the pledge raised its head again in, of all places, ethics class. I thought ethics was supposed to deal with hypothetical situations like what to do if two people are trapped in a mine shaft with only enough air for one. My ethics professor, however, chose to deal with the issues that touched our lives for real, like that dumb pledge. We talked about it at great length. It was a dumb pledge we all agreed, repressive, unrealistic. It was there just to appease the wealthy, conservative alumni. It was a relic from the past. We all nodded, except the professor. He said, "You said you wouldn't do it, so don't do it." I really disliked him for saying that. It couldn't be that simple, could it? In retrospect I see that it was that simple. The justice (or injustice), stupidity, and repressiveness of the pledge were not the real issues. The issue was that I signed the thing; I made a promise. So it was up to me to keep it.

I have learned in the intervening years that one's spiritual health improves by keeping one's promises, even if those promises are a little dumb, even if no one expects you to keep them. It's not about how other people see you, it's about how you see yourself. To keep a promise without peer support, but because you said you would, enhances one's sense of self-ownership. You said you would do it. That makes it a worthwhile target.

Psalm 15 asks the question, "O LORD, who shall sojourn in thy tent? / Who shall dwell on thy holy hill?" (Ps. 15:1). One of the answers the psalmist gives to his own question is this, "Who swears to his own hurt and does not change" (Ps. 15:4b). In other words, God is pleased with people who keep their promises even if they've made dumb promises that end up causing them to suffer. As Paul pointed out, "Suffering produces endurance, and endurance produces character, and character produces hope" (Rom. 5:3–4).

I wonder how many people view church participation in those terms. To be a member of the United Methodist Church or, I suppose, any church, you make a promise in front of the congregation and in the presence of God to support the church with, among other things, your presence. In other words, you promise to go to church whether it's convenient or not. Yet, on any given Sunday, people will come . . . *if* it's not raining, *if* they don't have company, *if* they are not skiing, *if* their children are singing in the children's choir, and *if* the sermon promises to be a good one and not too long. So preachers and choir directors and organists work harder and harder to make sure that the quality of the program is such that people will keep coming. Does anyone come just because he or she promised to? The choir may be screechy, the organ may be out of tune, the preacher may be incomprehensible, but they will be there because it's their church and they promised God they would support it with their presence.

One of my seminary professors had a debilitating heart condition which left him very weak and tired much of the time. He told me once that even when he didn't feel well and couldn't participate fully, he tried to be in church because, he said, he believed that worship was an offering we made to God; if he wasn't there, the offering would be incomplete. That's discipline. God honors it, it enriches the lives of the others who are part of the fellowship, and it brings spiritual health to the one who exercises it. I believe that Professor Burtner "dwells on God's holy hill" because he has "sworn to his own hurt and did not change."

My wife and I, like most modern couples, work hard all day. Most evenings, after dinner, we put a log on the fire, settle into our favorite chairs surrounded by our pets, and watch an endless parade of mindless drivel on television. Sometimes we say to each another, "Let's sit and read for a while and leave the television off." Sometimes we actually do it, but mostly I forget my glasses, or she forgets her book, or it's the night when something good is on the tube. But I've noticed that on those rare occasions when we actually do it—keep our pledge to leave the television off and read—I go to bed feeling so much better about myself.

There is a loftiness about having sat and read that is quite different from what you feel after hours spent with your feet propped up in front of the television. The effect seems to be the same regardless of the quality of the book or the television program. If I read a cheap novel instead of watching a highly rated documentary, the effect is the same: loftiness instead of waste. I have come to the conclusion that the result has nothing to do with the quality of the programming or the amount of material likely to be retained from either medium. The effect is the result of discipline.

Television watching is easy, it's habitual, and everyone does it *and* expects everyone else to do it. Yet to leave it off and read requires discipline. The sense of loftiness comes from having resisted the course of least resistance, taking the road less traveled, deciding to do something different, something not usual or expected, and then following through on that decision. It's an emotional high not unlike that which regular exercisers claim for themselves.

That high may not be so much a physiological phenomenon as it is a spiritual one, deriving from a challenge met, suffering endured, and a promise kept. That's discipline. For the marathon runner, the "high" comes not from winning, but from finishing. To make a promise and keep it, that's discipline and that's a real spiritual high. Those who understand that can begin to understand some of the other disciplines in the Bible: fasting, prayer, self-denial, and sacrifice.

When I was in high school, I used to tease my Catholic friends about their weird custom of giving up something for Lent. We Protestants represented a more enlightened, modern version of Christianity that didn't have to give up anything, not our possessions, not our pride, not our self-righteousness. We kept them all, even at Lent. So I would smile smugly as I said to Mike, Phyllis, and the others, "What are you giving up for Lent?" I didn't understand what the tradition meant, but then neither did they. Every year Mike gave up swearing and Phyllis gave up chocolate, things that they should have given up anyhow, things that were bad for them. The key is to give up something that's good for you. Lent is not an excuse to start a diet; it's a time to experience the joy of discipline and the growth that comes from suffering and self-denial.

Jesus was able to defeat Satan in the temptation story because of His discipline. He had the discipline of studying Scripture and the discipline of patience, and the devil went away defeated. There is a story in the gospels of a child possessed by a demon that the disciples could not cast out. Finally Jesus had to perform the exorcism Himself, and He reprimanded His disciples for their lack of faith. Then He added, "This kind never comes out except by prayer and fasting" (Matt. 17:21). Faith and power over evil come by way of discipline, making promises and then keeping them.

Fasting is an excellent example of denying ourselves that which is good for us. Indeed, food is essential to life. In our time, we see fasting used as a protest or a means to apply political pressure (a media-encouraged blackmail), but seldom is it viewed as a discipline or a gateway to spiritual vitality and health. When one denies oneself legitimate physical needs like food, one's attention becomes focused on the spiritual self and there is a resultant spiritual euphoria. Fasting and prayer are a dynamic duo in the quest for spiritual health and power.

Volumes have been written about prayer, what it is, how it works. Does prayer change God's mind, or does prayer change us? Why should we tell God what He already knows, being omniscient, and why should we tell God what He ought to be doing? These are questions that others have addressed eloquently, and I will not pursue them here. Let me say only that the primary function of prayer is obedience; it is an act of discipline. All through the Bible we are commanded to pray, even to pray without ceasing. Our Lord even instructed us as to the form of prayer (The Lord's Prayer) and offered Himself as a glorious example by praying often and passionately. We who call ourselves His disciples pray primarily because our Lord has commanded us to do so. It's an act of obedience and discipline. There is spiritual power to be gained by setting some specific times and places for prayer and then sticking to it, convenient or not. It doesn't matter if we understand it, or even if it works. We pray because Jesus prayed and we who call Him Lord follow His example.

Disciplines are most beneficial if observed in such a way that they cost something, something good. Suppose rather than giving a few dollars of your surplus to help feed the poor and then forgetting about it until tax time, you covered that donation with self-sacrifice. Suppose for every $20 you gave to a hunger program, you vowed to trim $20 out of your personal food budget. That might mean eliminating that favorite night out for dinner or buying hamburger rather than steak. Instead of buying frozen dinners, you would have to buy the cheaper raw ingredients and prepare them yourself. Thus the act of charity would also be an act of discipline and sacrifice as good for your spirit as it is for someone else's stomach.

I visited a church in Bakersfield once and stayed with a family who had made a pledge during Lent to live on a dollar a day each for food. They wanted to experience something of what people in the rest of the world experienced all year round. What must it be like, not to starve, but to go to bed hungry all the time? So their purchasing and measuring was done with great precision, right down to counting the pieces of macaroni. Sometimes one of them would splurge on a 95¢ breakfast that made the rest of the day's meals pretty sparse. The meal I shared with them consisted of spaghetti without sauce and a single saltine cracker.

The thing that impressed me most about their pledge was not that they had made it, but that they didn't abandon it because they were having company. That would have been the socially acceptable, even polite thing to do; everyone would agree to that. You can't really offer a houseguest unadorned spaghetti for dinner. But they did and didn't apologize for it. I admired that. They had sworn to their own hurt and did not change. They made a pledge for Lent and kept it, reaping immeasurable spiritual richness from the experience both as individuals and as a family. That's discipline.

Disciplined people do some things just because they are good for them, even if there is some pain involved in the doing. They do some things simply because our Lord has commanded it and some things just because they promised to do them. Some things they do just to prove to themselves that they are in control of their own selves, the masters of their fate, the captains of their souls.

I can only summarize by going back to the premise underlying all of this conjecture and commentary. There is a certain self-fulfilling quality about life: you tend to get what you expect and end up where you are headed. People with strong self-images and healthy spirits set high goals, have good, loving relationships, and have both fun and hard work in their lives. Remember the hair-coloring commercial on television where the woman says, "I'm worth it." Set lofty goals, then eagerly embrace the joy and the suffering that achieving these goals may bring. You're worth it!

Target fixation is a real phenomenon in your spiritual life. So set the target for your life and decide where you will land. If your targets require some "U" turns (repentance), so be it.

Finally, this. My high school commencement speaker asked us, the class of '61, to visualize the person we would be in twenty years. He paused for a moment while we each constructed our mental images. We expected him to come back to the microphone saying that if we worked hard enough, like Abe Lincoln, we could be that person. Instead he said, "That's the person you are now."

The goals and values that are your targets also define you now. When I lifted that forty-five-pound conglomeration of aluminum and nylon and ran down the hill, the target of red canvas in the middle of the green pasture was ultimate reality for me before my feet touched it; indeed, before my feet left the ground at the beginning of the flight. It became my ultimate reality when I became focused on it. It defined who I was at the moment in time that it became my target.

The future is now, the destination and the launching point are the same. We are who we hope to be someday. Let us hope and pray our targets are worthy.

- On a scale from 1 to 10, how well do you like yourself? Get that number up to at least a 7 (you get several points just by virtue of being a unique individual created in the image of God), then set some high and lofty goals for your life. You're worth it!

- You have choices, and choices add meaning to life. Take charge of your choices. Happy landing!

8

Blessed Are the Gentle Dweebs, the Late Bloomers, and the Hopelessly Average

It's a common axiom in our society that life begins at forty. No one explains or defends its veracity; we just recite it as if it were absolute, unmitigated, universal truth, and thus requires no defense. Since there is no companion literature, just the raw statement, all you can do is wait around for four decades or so to find out if it's true or not from personal experience. Then you have to decide in what way it's true. It can't be true in a purely physical sense; deterioration has already set in. That doesn't mean you can't look and feel good at forty, but you know that the forces that will ultimately take you down to dust are already irrevocably in place. It's just a matter of time. Whoopi Goldberg commented once that she was never going to do a nude scene in a movie because she was at that stage in her life where "gravity had her." There is no question that at forty the body starts to turn against you.

I had 20/20 vision my whole life until I went to the Department of Motor Vehicles to renew my driver's license on my fortieth birthday. With both eyes open I was fine. The man behind the counter said, "Read the smallest print you can." I said, "Acme Eye Chart Company, Cincinnati, Ohio. Patent pending." He didn't think that was funny. I wasn't surprised. I've noticed over the years that the DMV doesn't hire people who are long on humor. When I took another run at the eye chart with just my left eye open, was

I shocked! I said to the man, "I can't be absolutely sure, but I think it's an E." He didn't think that was funny either.

I was forty years old and needed glasses. I didn't think that was funny. For most of my life I didn't even need health insurance, but those days were past. The body begins to shut down ever so gradually. By forty you know it's true. I think I know why God planned it like that: it's so you and I will realize what's really important and put some energy into the part of our being that will last. Life does not begin at forty in any physical sense, so it must be true in some other way.

I think I've figured it out, having passed that hallowed landmark several years ago and having given it ample reflection and contemplation. Forty is the age at which you realize that there are some things about yourself you are never going to fix. You have spent the first half of your life developing your character and your moral fiber as well as your social skills, vocabulary, table manners, and socially acceptable responses to a variety of stimuli. At forty, the truth comes home: not only that you aren't perfect, but you're not likely to achieve perfection in the last half of your life either. There you stand before the mirror of life, peering over your bifocals at the extra roll around your middle, facing for perhaps the first time that that's not only who you are, but who you are likely to remain. That flab exists in your mental and spiritual lives as well.

So you say, "The heck with it!" It's a perfectly liberating moment when you acknowledge your own imperfection and decide that everyone else is going to have to acknowledge it as well. "If they don't like me as I am with all my warts and imperfections, that's tough!" There is an amazing thing that happens when you reach that point; you loosen up, relax. You're more spontaneous and easygoing. People start to like you more. Your relationships improve. At the same time you begin to have a deeper appreciation of the fact that God, too, has accepted you with all your imperfections and loves you just like you are.

Life begins at forty because you have finally come to a place where you can accept and celebrate yourself without pretense or self-recrimination. You are free for perhaps the first time; free to be who you are. The second half of life looks very inviting.

So if you are a dweeb, a geek, or a nerd, it's okay. We have been done a great service by those television shows and movies that flash us back to the '50s and '60s and then up to the present. They underscore the truth that some of those people who were the worst nerds in school turned out to be the warmest, brightest, most successful adults. Some of them remain nerds, but that's okay, too. Perhaps life begins when you realize that your best friend is a nerd, but you love him anyway.

I was a painfully skinny kid when I was a teenager. Actually I have always been skinny, but it seemed more important during my teen years. I endured all those jokes about dancing around in the shower to get wet and wearing water skis in the bathtub to keep from going down the drain. In fact I did look like a skeleton with skin, and I knew it. My figure consisted of an Adams apple and two kneecaps. I liked basketball but hated the outfit that revealed my embarrassingly deficient physique to the world and to the cheerleaders. I hated the locker room scene, particularly the fact that I got the locker next to Gary Grant, whose arms were bigger than my legs.

At the age of sixteen, I actually went to the town doctor to ask him to help me gain some weight. He pointed out how glad I was going to be that I was trim when I got to be thirty. He called me trim—no one ever called me trim before, skinny or lanky, but never trim. Besides when you're sixteen, what do you care about being thirty? That's too far off in the future to imagine. But he was right, and at forty people admired my trim build and asked me my secret. I smile now and say, "Metabolism." When I was younger I hated this form, but now I feel really good about it. I'll bet Gary Grant looks like a blimp.

I was not only skinny and unathletic, but I had a dangerous gentle streak that was out of character in the rugged middle American farm town in which I lived. People went hunting, butchered hogs, chewed tobacco, and talked rough. They liked stock car races and tractor pulls. I liked music and art. I tried hunting but always harbored a secret hope that the squirrel would get away.

In 1951, we had a flood in eastern Kansas. When the water receded there were swarms of little fish left trapped in the ditches along the sides of the roads in the bottom land. Soon the ditches dried up and the fish died in the sun. I spent the better part of one day with a bucket and my bicycle, running rescue missions from the ditch to the river. Although my back ached, with every bucket of fish I released into the living stream of the river, there was a strange surge of something like joy and a sense of oneness with the world and with God, the Creator of both me and those little fish. To celebrate life, even such tiny life, is always to celebrate yourself. Someone has said, "Gentleness in men does not blur the line between men and women, it sharpens the line between men and beasts."

There you have it, the confessions of a gentle dweeb, a skinny, unathletic, tender hearted kid who didn't grow up so bad and who at the age of forty knows some stuff about celebrating life.

But it's even worse. I was a late bloomer. Why do we always reward those people who are ahead of their age group and congratulate those who get to skip a grade? They are in danger of using up all the good experiences in life before they're old enough to appreciate them properly.

Ronny Means was the only kid in my first grade class to flunk. We all laughed at old dumb Ronny Means. Ronny would always be one year behind the rest of us in school. I felt differently about Ronny when athletics became important to us all. Ronny was one year behind his class but one year ahead in coordination and physical maturity. He had a one-year advantage on everyone. By the time he was a high school senior, he was a town star in both basketball and football. Life's adventures are too luscious to rush. Go slow. Enjoy.

That's what I tell teens who are discovering their sexuality and trying to cope with the sexual mores of their peers. They want to know when they should engage in sexual intercourse. I tell them to go slow and enjoy. If they rush it, they might miss all the good stuff along the way. Enjoy hand holding as long as possible, the first kiss, the courting, the flirting, and the surprising emotional and physiological responses your body dishes out. Savor it. If you're the last person in the world to become sexually active, good for you! That may mean that you won't get bored with it as soon as others do. In that great movie, *The Last Picture Show*, the mother says to her daughter (whom she has rescued from the motel in the nick of time), "Everything gets old if you do it often enough."

I didn't marry until I was forty-two. While others are bored with sex and their wives or are perhaps on their second or third marriage, I can still be surprised and challenged in the early stages of my first marriage. I'm a middle-aged newlywed experiencing some marvelous things at a time in life when I am prepared to appreciate and enjoy them.

Life begins at forty or at any age when we can take an honest look at ourselves like we are and say, "That's good."

I've saved the worst word for last. The word is *average*. No one wants to be average. In the movie *All That Jazz*, Joe Gideon works himself so hard he ends up flat on his back with a heart attack. A performer from a movie he is producing comes to his bedside. "I have insight into you, Joe Gideon," he says. "You're afraid you're not special. You're afraid you're really average." It's the story of a man who worked himself to death to keep from being average.

As I've mentioned, in most sports I would have to invest lots of patience and practice even to achieve the rank of average. Needless to say, whether I'm holding a tennis racquet or a golf club, I get beat a lot. Once in Anchorage, Alaska, I played racquetball with an opponent who was eager to play me again. I explained that my plane was leaving the next day. "Perhaps in the morning, before you go to the airport . . . ," he insisted. I inquired why he was so persistent, couldn't he find anyone else to play with? "Yes," he replied. "But you're the only person I can beat."

I never did mind much getting beat. What I do mind is not playing my best. If someone else's best is better than mine, that's fine. If, however, for some reason I'm unable to come up with my best game, it makes me furious. Once I went to deliver a lecture without allowing enough time for preparation. The audience thought it was great; I was miserable. I was not at my best. Once I went to perform a concert, but was fatigued from lack of sleep. I couldn't give it all the energy it needed. The audience was satisfied; I wasn't. I wasn't my best.

The surprise blessing of being average is that it teaches you to give it your best. If you are naturally superior, you can coast. If you have to struggle just to stay even, you know the joy of giving a project your absolute best shot and emerging victorious.

There is something wonderfully liberating about knowing you gave it your best shot, even if the shot misses. Those of us who know the panic of discovering we are average (I slid through college on a 2.4 GPA) also know the joy of giving everything we attempt our absolute best.

This is one of my favorite stories. I heard it years ago on the "Merv Griffin Show" and I hope my retelling of it does justice to it. It was told by Eydie Gorme, the nightclub singer and performer, after she had just sung one of those passionate torch songs she does so well. The host asked her who her role models were and how she got started in show business. She said her idol was Judy Garland. She had patterned her style, her voice, even her hairdo after Judy Garland. Then she told this story.

She said her first big break came when she got the chance to play the Waldorf-Astoria in New York. The enthusiastic audience packed the place every night. The critics gave her rave reviews. She was on her way to the big time.

The next engagement was in Pittsburgh, but not actually in Pittsburgh, it was an outlying suburb off a state highway. It wasn't really a Class A nightclub, like the Waldorf. It was more of a roadhouse with beer signs flashing in the window and a pool table in the back. The showroom was small and tacky, and there was a little five-piece band there to accompany her. To make matters worse, there was a blizzard on her opening night, and only a few semi-sober patrons drifted in to hear her sing.

The next night the blizzard got worse; she didn't even make it to the club. The manager called to inform her that if she didn't sing, she didn't get paid. She asked if anyone else had made it. He said "No, but that's beside the point."

The third night she had to bribe a taxi driver to take her out to that roadhouse. There were the manager, three members of the five-piece band, and she. When it came time for her show, she gave the cue, the lights dimmed, the trio started to play her music, and she began to sing to an empty house. In the middle of her first song, the door opened and through the haze and the blinding spotlight she saw five shadowy figures come in and sit at a center table. She said she made up her mind that if she could sing to a packed house in New York, she could sing to five people in a Pittsburgh roadhouse.

She said she sang that night with a clarity and a passion and an energy that were as good as any time in her life. She sang her best for those five strangers out in the dark. When her show was over, the spotlight went out, the houselights came up, she looked out at that table, four of the people she didn't recognize, but the fifth seated among them was Judy Garland. She couldn't believe her eyes. Of all the people in the world she would love to meet and sing for, Judy Garland was on the top of her list. There she was, in, of all places, a Pennsylvania roadhouse in the middle of a blizzard.

Such a lovely story hardly needs any application. To celebrate yourself, even if you are average, a late bloomer, a slow learner, or just a dweeb, is to give it your best shot every time. Sometimes it really pays off and you entertain angels unaware. We must celebrate every moment, even the little ones. We must give our best to every task, even insignificant ones, even if very few take notice.

There is a commercial that says, "You only go through life once, so you have to grab for all the gusto you can." If ever a commercial deserved an "Amen," that one does.

Most of us are not good at clever, off-the-top-of-our-heads answers. My most embarrassing moment is when someone asks me, "What was your most embarrassing moment?" and I can't think of anything. I usually think of just the right comeback when I reenact the scene in the shower the next morning. Of course, when I tell about it later, I tell it the way it happened in the shower. But once in a while the things you say off the top of your head sound pretty good, even in retrospect. In fact, after much thought and several showers, you discover that you can't improve on it at all. I have two such experiences to share and in a way they are quite similar.

My college newspaper had a column that was simply a list of responses of random students to various semi-interesting but nonthreatening questions. Since much of this journalistic investigation was done between classes, there wasn't much time for considered answers. The question that was tossed to me on the way to English Literature was, "What do you fear more than anything else?" My snap answer—"Missing something." Years later in a religious forum, I was asked what was the worst sin I could imagine? I answered, "Wearing shoes on the beach." Upon further reflection I've decided that both answers are perfect. Given the opportunity to change them, I would choose to let them stand.

Both questions and answers were about experience. My biggest fear is to miss an experience, to have an opportunity laid before me and to pass it by out of fear or caution or peer consciousness, not to do something that might bring joy and adventure and a new dimension to life. What if it were at my doorstep, and I passed it by? That would be a tragedy! And that semi-serious comment about shoes on the beach: to insulate your feet so that you can't feel the radiant heat of the sun or the little granules as they mold to the shape of your feet and squirt up between your toes, to pass up an experience like that—free and joyous—for fear of stepping on a piece of glass or tracking sand into the car, that was indeed the worst behavior I could imagine.

Why should we allow ourselves to experience such a narrow slice of life? The world is a gigantic pie. We nibble around the edges for fear of being accused of gluttony. The healthy, beautiful spirit samples broadly from the smorgasbord of emotions and experiences. There are no speed limits on the freeway of life (if I may change the metaphor from food to horsepower). If you are a sports car that can go from 0 to 180, why would you choose to cruise at 55 all the time? If you go too fast or too slow, it may make others uncomfortable, but it's your car and your road. What's it going to be— celebration or conformity?

The word *appropriate* may be the most damning word in the English language. I've spent my life learning appropriate behavior, table manners, greetings and responses, and dress, only to discover that the people who interest me the most are the ones who care the least about so-called appropriate behavior.

When I was a child I was trained that it was not appropriate for me to play with dolls or cry. I liked dolls. I also liked trucks, so I hauled my dolls around in the back of my trucks. Crying was another issue. No one ever came right out and said I shouldn't do it, but in a thousand ways that message got communicated. It was inappropriate behavior for men. If there is laughter and weeping, dolls and trucks, why not embrace them all? Why settle for the bland, safe, middle ground? There's more on the smorgasbord than white bread and iced tea. Nothing will make you feel so alive as a real honest-to-goodness belly laugh or the experience of water welling up in your eyes, the itchy tracks that run down your cheeks, and the salt taste of the tears on your tongue. Not to experience that and all of life's variety is to wear shoes on the beach, to insulate oneself from the temperature and texture of life. To miss the life that is all around us would indeed be the worst sin of all. So, blessed are the slow starters and the incurably average who have to rush to keep up and who have to scream to be noticed. At least we experience rushing and screaming, and our hearts beat faster for it.

Jesus surrounded Himself with the gentle dweebs, the late bloomers, and the average types who could be infused with the zest for life. Being slow learners, it took them a long time to catch on to the idea. But when they finally did, they changed the world. God still draws primarily from that pool for His most blessed workers.

I recently heard the dean of the chapel of Harvard Divinity School tell about that campus being visited by Archbishop Desmond Tutu and Mother Theresa during the same semester. He said that there were some striking similarities between them. These were his words: "They were both noticeably average and genuinely surprised that God had chosen to use them."

So I say again, blessed are the gentle dweebs, the late bloomers, and the hopelessly average. Not only I have said it, the Bible has said it:

> Blessed are the poor in spirit, . . .
>
> Blessed are those who mourn, . . .
>
> Blessed are the meek, . . .
>
> Blessed are those who hunger and thirst for righteousness, . . .
>
> Blessed are the merciful, . . .
>
> Blessed are the pure in heart, . . .
>
> Blessed are the peacemakers, . . .
>
> *Matt. 5:3–9*

The healthy spirit acknowledges who he or she is, accepts it as a blessing, then reaches for the feast of life with both hands.

> Take a good honest look at yourself and then like what you see.

9

Mirrors and Windows

Mirrors and windows are both made of glass and are both commonly found in most homes, but they have functions that are exactly opposite. While windows remind us that there is a world out there, mirrors are designed to enable us to focus on ourselves. The healthy spirit, like a window, is not preoccupied with self, but with the world beyond self. Selfishness may be the ugliest spiritual trait imaginable, while nothing beautifies the spirit quite like generosity and self-giving.

Israel Goldstein said, "I believe that the deepest and most abiding satisfactions of life come not from receiving but from giving." It's not an original concept but one that, once discovered, is intensely profound. So we are generous not just because it's good for other people who are the beneficiaries of our generosity, but because it's good for our own spiritual well-being and happiness.

In his book *The Conquest of Happiness*, Bertrand Russell says:

> I was not born happy. As a child, my favorite hymn was: "Weary of earth and laden with sin." . . . In adolescence, I hated life and was continually on the verge of suicide, from which, however, I was restrained by the desire to know more mathematics. Now, on the contrary, I enjoy life; I might almost say that with every year that passes I enjoy it more . . . very largely it is due to diminishing preoccupation with myself. Like others who had a Puritan

106

education, I had a habit of meditating on my sins, follies and shortcomings. I seemed to myself—no doubt justly—a miserable specimen. Gradually I learned to be indifferent to myself and my deficiencies; I came to center my attention upon external objects: the state of the world, various branches of knowledge, individuals for whom I felt affection.

So it's good to be generous, even if you do it for selfish reasons. Being other-oriented is good for you. It brings healing, self-worth, and joy to your life that self-preoccupation can never accomplish. It takes the attention off yourself. Turn your mirrors into windows. There is a world out there that wants your love and affection. Offer it and it will enrich your spirit.

There is an old Chinese tale about a woman whose son was killed. She went to the village holy man and asked, "Can you make a potion that will make the pain go away?" The holy man said, "Yes, but first you must bring me a loaf of bread from the home of one who has never known pain." So she went to the rich neighborhood, knocked on the first door she came to, and made her request. The woman at the first house said, "I would like to help you, but you have come to the wrong house. I, too, have known pain, for my son was also killed." They consoled each other, and the woman moved on to the next house. The reply was the same, "This house has also known pain." The same with the next and the next. At the end of the day the woman still did not have her loaf of bread for the holy man, but somehow through all the sharing and caring and consoling, she found that her pain was eased. A miraculous healing was taking place. The holy man knew that the woman herself held the key to the magic of healing. It was in the act of self-giving and caring about others that her own healing was accomplished.

For ten years I directed a church singles program in San Diego. There were people there who had lost spouses by death or divorce. There were people who had never married and, with their biological clocks ticking away, were beginning to wonder why marriage had passed them by. There were lots of people with legitimate needs and real pain. What did we do with those people? We didn't focus our attention on our own neediness. We took food to a Tijuana orphanage and gave a Valentine's party at an old people's home. We focused on the needs of others, and a miracle happened in terms of our own legitimate needs.

To be other-oriented is to gain the ultimate benefit for oneself. It's one of the grand paradoxes of life. As the children's song goes, "Love is nothing till you give it away. You end up having more." That's why we say it's more blessed to give than to receive, because the act of giving blesses the giver more than being on the receiving end. Jesus taught that people reap what they sow. That means that what you hand out is what you will get back. It's one of those simple truths that we tend not to take seriously because it doesn't sound all that profound and we've heard it since childhood. *A rolling stone gathers no moss.* . . . *A stitch in time saves nine.* . . . *You reap what you sow.* Separate that last one out. Get it off the plaque on your wall and into your heart. *You reap what you sow!* I can't count the number of times a person has sat in my office and complained, "No one likes me. No one listens to me. No one wants to be my friend." My response is always, "Do you like anyone? Do you listen to anyone? Do you try to be friendly with anyone?" They are the personification of that old song that goes, "I ain't never got nothing from no body, and I don't intend to do nothing for no body, no how."

Bill came to tell me that he was leaving San Diego because no one was friendly. He had been coming to my church as a last resort, and he wanted me to know that no one here was friendly either. I assumed that he was one of those recent transplants from back East who left the warmth of long-established friendships at home and was not quite prepared for the homesickness and sense of loss that people experience when they're trying to get established in a new city. So I asked him how long he had been in San Diego. He said, "Seventeen years." Seventeen years and no one was friendly? I convinced him to try again for at least one more month, and I kept an eye on him.

We have a reception after our worship services called the Coffee Chat. (That title pretty well describes what goes on there.) Bill stood flat against the back wall, arms crossed in front of him like a barrier, and a scowl engraved firmly on his face. "No one was friendly," he said, and he was right. The next week, the scene repeated itself: same wall, same stance, same expression. I said, "Hi, Bill," took him by the arm and introduced him to a circle of people standing nearby. They smiled; he smiled. The conversation began. I left. He is still coming to church and often in the company of an attractive lady he met one day at Coffee Chat. It can't be that simple, can it?

The tragic irony is that it often is that simple. I wish it were more complicated, then you wouldn't feel so dumb for missing it, but it's not. The magic is in the simplicity: What you dish out is what you get back. If you care about, heal, and bless others, they will care about, heal, and bless you.

I've proven this theory in some of the toughest test markets in America. Take the city of brotherly love, for example, a place where I've had a pretty negative experience (remember the van? the guitar?). It was a rainy Saturday when I set out determined to walk the length and breadth of that historic city to trace the footprints of both Benjamin Franklin and Rocky Balboa. Keep in mind that many Eastern cities take pride in their rudeness. In New York, swearing and pounding on car hoods seems to be a way of life. In Boston traffic, there are no rules except for one: he who has the most fenders knocked off, goes first. In California, on the other hand, a pedestrian can step off the curb, even between crosswalks, and the traffic will actually stop. That's hard for Easterners to believe.

As you move east across the country, you should be more and more careful about trying that. By the time you reach Philadelphia, you will want to look both ways twice before you step off the curb even in a crosswalk with a walk signal beckoning you. On a particularly aggressive day, like when the moon is full or when it's raining, cars will actually come up on the sidewalk and try to pick you off.

That's the kind of setting into which I carried my theory about being nice to people and their being nice back. After a couple of hours of dodging traffic, I made a pit stop at a storefront restaurant. You know the kind: checkered oilcloth tablecloths, tables that never seem to sit straight (someone put a matchbook under one leg), plastic candleholders on the table, and paper flowers caked with dust. The menus were laminated, with masking tape over the prices and new prices written in. When I opened it up, someone else's jelly was in the fold.

The waitress held her order book in front of her face and barked, "What do you want?" I thought to myself, here is a woman who needs to hear a kind word and a cheerful greeting. So with all the glee I could muster, I said, "Don't you just love it when it rains? It makes everything smell so fresh." She grumbled, "I'll come back when you know what you want." Sometimes the magic takes longer to work than other times.

When she finally returned, I cast all restraint aside and went straight for the heart: "How do you keep your hair looking so nice on such a rainy day?" Her voice rose two octaves and her face beamed like Shirley Temple's on the Good Ship Lollipop. "I just have to use a little more hair spray," she said as she fluffed her hair with her hand. After that I couldn't get rid of her. I had a pile of little jelly containers fetched from her apron pocket and she overflowed my coffee cup several times. She wanted more! It can't be that simple, but it is. If you care about other people and show it, the blessings that come back to you are innumerable.

There is an unfortunately designed freeway interchange in San Diego. The traffic comes off of one freeway onto the next at the beginning of a steep hill. The route is also used by the trucks from the local cement plant. The result is that traffic traveling at freeway speeds gets backed up behind cement trucks going twenty miles per hour or less. It's dangerous at worst, frustrating at best.

My wife got behind one of those big yellow-and-red cement trucks. She had to watch the tire tread to be sure the truck was actually moving. It was an ordeal of several minutes before the truck took the exit, which was also her exit. At the end of the exit, she pulled up beside the truck, fuming. She glanced over and up at the driver who was looking at her. Then a hand puppet appeared in his window. It was one of the Sesame Street characters, and it waved and the driver smiled.

The driver knew the kind of consternation he caused other drivers. It was a situation that couldn't be helped, but he could offer a smile and a kind of apology, and he went out of his way to find a way to do so. He had given a little something to my wife, and all her tension immediately dissipated. She confessed to me that she still drives around looking for yellow-and-red cement trucks.

The great spirits around you are the ones who know that magic. They are always getting awards and accolades for what the world calls their generosity, but they don't do it for a plaque and a dinner thrown in their honor. They see their other-orientation almost like an investment, and they know they get back far more than they ever give away.

I suppose I learned that truth for the first time when I went away to college. I didn't decide to enroll until two weeks before classes began. So I packed my Plymouth with all my earthly possessions and was off to Oklahoma with $40 in my pocket. Halfway through the first semester, I got a check in the mail for $150 from a couple in my hometown. They weren't relatives, they weren't even Methodists, but they had sent me what seemed at the time an incredible amount of money. I wrote them a grateful thank-you letter and said, "Of course when I'm able, I'll pay the money back." Their response came in terms that were firm and almost harsh: "Don't you dare pay that money back and rob us of the joy of giving!"

Nearly ten years later, I was at a senior high summer camp in California. I had just left a church position in June and would be beginning another job in September. In the meantime, I survived by eating lots of camp food. This camp had a tradition. Every year all the kids would pool their money, and a counselor would go to town and buy Cokes and cookies for a Friday night farewell party. The word got around camp that I was without income for several months *and* out of gas money, with a trip to Ohio facing me. So they took up a collection that came to over $100. It was the money for the Friday night party. My first impulse was to take some of the money and buy some Cokes and cookies; then I heard a little voice say, "Don't rob them of the joy of giving." On Friday night we had the party. The refreshment was water, served in little paper cups and some dry crackers scavenged from the camp kitchen. That was it. They say it was the best farewell party ever. They had experienced, perhaps for the first time, the joy of sacrificial giving. They had sacrificed self-interest for generosity; they had turned their mirrors into windows and the experience had bound them together in a way that can only be described as spiritual. Those little cups of water and crumbly wafers constituted for us what communion was meant to be; not a solemn ritual, but a celebration of mutual self-giving.

Even in the church, of all places, we are in danger of losing the truth of the principle and the companion joy—we have started to ask people to give what they can afford. Jesus taught that only sacrificial giving is efficacious. We must not only give until it hurts; we should give until it feels good—give until the magic begins to work, give until we experience the magic of giving.

There is a special magic about giving oneself in concern for the needs of others, and it is particularly potent when the opportunity comes in the midst of one's own desperate need. I was at an Easter Seals camp in Big Bear, California. All the kids were handicapped. Some were blind, some deaf, some in wheelchairs, many with multiple handicaps. You haven't really lived until you've had a water gun fight with fifty blind kids or danced with someone in a wheelchair.

We were at the dining table. The kid next to me in a wheelchair had some ailment that robbed him of most of his muscle control and slurred his speech. He fed himself by scooping up a handful of food and throwing it in the general direction of his mouth. No one laughed. After dinner he turned to me and with great difficulty mumbled out these words, "Reverend Morley, do you believe in prayer?" My heart nearly stopped. A thousand thoughts raced through my mind in the seconds that seemed like hours. What would I say? Does he want me to pray that he get up out of his chair and walk? Should I point out that even Jesus didn't heal everyone? Should I say that his infirmity makes him strong and that someday he'll find meaning in it? How would I know that? All those thoughts passed through my mind during a single breath. I said, "Yes, I believe in prayer." And he said, "Will you pray for my counselor? He's deaf." There was a great, wise, healthy spirit in that crippled little body. He had learned the magic. In the midst of his own desperate need, he would have me pray for others. I never pray for myself now without thinking of him and thanking God for his ministry to me.

What made that experience all the more stark was the fact that I went immediately from there to what I call the rich kids' scuba diving camp. Everyone there was tanned and healthy, the kind of kids we all want ours to be. They paid no attention to me and very little to one another as they ran down to the warm sandy beach in their OP swim trunks and Ferrari sunglasses.

It didn't take me long to figure out who had the healthy spirit.

Of course, one doesn't have to be crippled to have that kind of concern for others, but have you noticed how often it's true? I have gone to hospitals to comfort the dying and gone away having been comforted by them. They say that when people go blind, their other senses are improved. Perhaps when people's bodies let them down, they develop great spirits. Perhaps that's why God lets us all get wounded once in a while—to give us an opportunity to trust the magic, to sow kindness, caring, and healing in this world and then be ready to reap what we have sown.

Paul talks a lot about sowing: "Whatever a man sows, that he will also reap" (Gal. 6:7). "The point is this: he who sows sparingly will also reap sparingly, and he who sows bountifully will also reap bountifully" (2 Cor. 9:6). But the New Testament doesn't have a corner on the sowing market. The Old Testament also speaks of the mystery and the magic. "He who is kind to the poor lends to the LORD, / and he will repay him for his deed" (Prov. 19:17).

Give up self-preoccupation. Move away from the mirror and toward the window. There is a world out there that wants your blessing and wants to bless you. There is a magic about self-giving, so let that magic be the secret potion that beautifies and enriches your spirit. The promise of the Bible is that if we will care for the needs of others, God will care for our needs. To move closer to other people, particularly the needy of the world, is to move closer to God. "As you did it to one of the least of these my brethren, you did it to me" (Matt. 25:40).

> Focus your attention on the needs and well-being of other people and forget about your own. Do it intentionally. There is someone you know right now who needs your love, affirmation, time. Offer it. It's even better if you have to give up something you had planned for yourself. The next time you find yourself dwelling on your own needs and interests, call up the Salvation Army or the Heart Association or your church and ask how you can help. Don't forget to measure the joy that comes back to you.

10

Travel Light

All of us have too much stuff. Just look around your house at the stuff you have that you haven't noticed in years, not to mention the stuff that's hidden away in boxes in attics, cellars, and drawers. Life, for many, is a process of accumulating and storing stuff. You know you have passed all the limits of sanity in the quest for stuff when, come moving time, you discover a dozen boxes of stuff you didn't unpack from the last time you moved. So you just move it again.

After a while, stuff starts to take on an intrinsic value simply by virtue of having been moved so many times. The first time I moved, I decided to get really organized and label all my boxes, particularly the things that I would need to find immediately at the next place, things like towels, dishes, etc. I moved thirty-five boxes; only eight were labeled. The rest was just stuff.

The trouble with having so much stuff is that the more stuff you have, the more time and energy you spend maintaining, organizing, and protecting it. You have to have a larger house in which to store it. You need an alarm system so no one will get your stuff. And, of course, you need sufficient insurance so you can always replace your stuff. When you are a big-time stuff collector, you build security fences and hire guards and guard dogs. If your stuff is really valuable, you lock it in a safe deposit box and have false stuff made just like it so people will know you have the real stuff somewhere.

What happens to all that stuff when you die? Your kids will fight over it. The lawyers will get most of it. And the Salvation Army will get the rest. You see, some old stuff becomes antiques and some old stuff just stays old stuff. It's hard to tell which is which, so you just keep it all.

I used to live in a neighborhood where I was burglarized about every six months. The last time the thieves broke in, they didn't take anything, they probably looked around and said, "Our stuff is better that this stuff!" That's how you know you are getting down to an acceptable level, when you don't have anything left worth stealing. Since then, I've moved to a safer neighborhood and my stuff is proliferating again.

If you will lighten your load, it will lighten your spirit. That truth is gathered in poetic form in the reading that was released on a record album called "Celestial Navigations":

> I reached the top of the hill in good shape. The sun was coming up at my back and casting a warm glow on the hills beyond. I knew this was the place that I had been looking for because there, looking like a blue velvet ribbon that had dropped from a goddess's hair, was the river, winding through the bottom of the valley. I could hear the birds singing their first songs of the day. Crack of the twig and a deer was staring at me through the bushes. I turned and ran back down to where I'd left my things more or less in a pile under some giant pine trees, boxes and trunks and bags and suitcases, containers of all shapes and sizes. I looked at this mountain of belongings and thought, "What is all this stuff that I keep carting from one place to the next?" I wondered if I would need it, so I opened the largest box. In it was all my childhood, a pair of baby shoes, Teddy bear, an old blue blanket, a tooth that I had lost when I was five years old, a note passed in class to my first girlfriend, and on and on . . .
>
> No, I thought, I won't need this stuff in that valley. I won't have time for memories, so I closed the box up and pushed it aside. Then a very strange thing happened. My back got straighter and I grew a foot taller. No, it must be my imagination. I opened the largest trunk. In it was all my beauty, an old painting I loved, a piece of sculpture, a broken guitar, books I knew by heart, my first

poems, a shell collection, and on and on. . . . No, I thought, I won't need this stuff in that valley. There there is beauty enough and it is alive, so I closed the trunk up and pushed it aside. No it was not my imagination, I grew another foot taller and a gray film washed off my body like tears and my senses were suddenly flooded with the beauty of my surroundings. I kicked aside a paper bag full of canned goods and recipes and grew another foot taller. I picked up a valise full of philosophical musings, sociological clauses and political speeches and flung them away with vengeance and suddenly felt completely guiltless and sure of myself and grew another foot taller. Then I dug a large hole and except for one small box, I shoved everything in the hole and buried it all forever. I was now so tall and alive that the giant pine trees just grazed the palms of my hands. The small box had grown too, in it were some tools and a flute. I picked them up and took them with me, for they are the things of the future, and started up the hill. I gazed out over my new world and it was all right because it was as large and open as I was. I looked back once, and there far below me on the grave of my past was a new bright tiny yellow flower waving peacefully in the morning breeze. Then I turned and forgot and walked happily into the valley.

If life is a journey, then he who travels best, travels light. All of the great holy men, from Buddha to Gandhi, and including Jesus, have warned against the accumulation of stuff. But we are given mixed signals in this country because austerity flies in the face of the American way of life. We are valued in this nation not only by what we produce but by what we consume. We receive thousands of signals and bits of information every day through advertising, all trying to convince us to buy more stuff.

The point was brought home to me in 1982 when I visited the Soviet Union. Up to that time, I had assumed that the Soviet people were enjoying roughly a similar lifestyle to us. If they could match us in their space program, they could probably match us on earth. I found the people to be very friendly and quite curious about Americans and how we live. They asked about my house. At that time I lived in a small one-bedroom Spanish-style home. I left "Spanish-style" out of my description because I didn't think I could explain what that meant. They nodded and said, "So, you have one room." "No, actually, I also have a living room, a kitchen, and a bathroom besides the one bedroom." I remember when I moved into that little house, one of my friends actually cried because it was so small and humble. Yet these people were amazed that one person could occupy all that space. Then they asked if I had a car. I was a bit embarrassed because I had two cars. I couldn't tell them that one was an old MG and so didn't count.

Through the centuries there have been many apocalyptic visions of the final judgment. Mine is a little more mundane than most; it comes in the form of a dream. It's like standing in line at the checkout stand at Safeway or going through international customs at the airport. You have heard it said that you can't take it with you; in my dream, our judgment is that you have to take it with you—all of it!

How many of those little carts will it take to haul all that stuff you have spent a lifetime accumulating? Every time you go back to move the rest of your carts forward, someone with less stuff cuts in line. But this is the worst part: you not only have to take it all with you, you have to explain and justify it all. The angel at the turnstile will ask what this is and why it is so important that you have dragged it around with you all these years. So I see myself standing there in line deciding what I will say about each thing.

Of course I have a lot of time to work on my explanation: the line is long, there is only one gate, and they are not computerized in Heaven—they still have to go through a big book. I just about have my story rehearsed to my satisfaction when I notice that I have one whole cart filled with nothing but shoes. I have brown shoes for my brown suits and black shoes for my black suits. I couldn't find any blue shoes for my blue suits, so I bought gray. There are casual shoes and dress-up shoes, winter shoes, summer shoes, rain shoes, and snow shoes and, of course, athletic shoes, lots of athletic shoes. You see you need different shoes depending on what sport you're playing. You can't wear black-soled shoes on the racquetball court; it says so on the door. You can't wear running shoes to play tennis, because those are for going forward, and tennis is a game where you run sideways. I've read enough articles about ankle injuries to know that you can't go forward in sideways shoes and vice versa. I just about have my explanation figured out for my cart full of shoes when I notice that the guy in line behind me is barefoot. Then I wake up.

On earth we may be measured by what we have, but on the other side we will be measured by what we give away, not by the greatness of our heap of stuff, but by the greatness of our spirit. Poverty doesn't guarantee a healthy spirit, but for those of us who have much, there is spiritual benefit to be gained by stifling our need to have more, by lightening our load. Give some of that stuff to those who have less and pay attention to the well-being and nurture of the spirit. It was Thoreau who said, "I make myself rich by wanting less."

Jesus said, "Do not lay up for yourselves treasures on earth, where moth and rust consume and where thieves break in and steal, but lay up for yourselves treasures in heaven, where neither moth nor rust consumes and where thieves do not break in and steal. For where your treasure is, there will your heart be also" (Matt. 6:19–21).

The issue of possessions (stuff) must always remain in the self-awareness of the church. Churches have stuff, lots of it. We own prime property often at the best intersections in the neighborhood. We build lovely, efficient, and comfortable buildings filled with stained glass, brass candlesticks, and padded pews. We invest in things that are aesthetically pleasing, as indeed we should. The church has always been a patron of the arts and should continue to be. If creativity is next to godliness, then all expressions thereof are of divine worth and spiritual value. The question for the church is not whether we will have stuff, but when we have stepped over that fuzzy line between aesthetic sensitivity and garish display, between the collections of art that uplift the spirit and the stuff that weighs it down.

I visited a church in Oklahoma. It was one of those cathedral-like downtown churches supported by lots of oil money. I was there the day they dedicated a new mosaic in the foyer of the church. They paid $100,000 for it. I know that because the price tag was mentioned several times during the dedication ceremony.

When it was over, I asked the pastor of the church that ongoing question. I didn't ask it as a criticism or a judgment, but because the question must always be asked in the church: "Was that the best possible stewardship of that $100,000?" He leaned back in his chair and said, "The people who come to this church are the upper crust of this city. They live in lovely homes, appreciate art, and travel the world over. They are very sophisticated. They aren't going to come to a storefront. Perhaps they will come here because of that mosaic and then hear the gospel. I can't preach to them if they don't come."

It was a good answer, and in general I agree with it. But I asked the next rhetorical question, not just for him, but for me and for all of us. "After you get them here with the $100,000 mosaic, can you then speak to them with integrity of the Carpenter from Nazareth who had no place to lay His head?"

That question goes unanswered. It must go unanswered because it must always remain as a question to haunt us, correct us, and call us back to the gospel story. To be a well spirit is to live your whole life asking that difficult question and its companions: How much is enough? At what point does my load of stuff begin to weigh down my spirit?

- Get rid of some stuff; sell it, give it away, throw it away.
- The next time you are tempted to buy something, don't.

11

The Childlike Spirit

Let it be very clear from the beginning that *childlikeness* and *childishness* bear no similarities at all except that they sound a little alike. Childlikeness refers to all those things of childhood that we ought to keep our whole life but usually lose around puberty. Childishness refers to those things that we ought to get rid of as soon as possible but usually keep as long as we live.

Jesus often spoke of childlikeness as a character trait. He called a child over to the disciples and said, "Unless you turn and become like children, you will never enter the kingdom of heaven. Whoever humbles himself like this child, he is the greatest in the kingdom of heaven" (Matt. 18:3–4). What traits could He have been referring to that grown men could adopt to make themselves great? I think He meant things like creativity, spontaneity, humility, trust, and joy over little things.

Creativity. When God created the universe, He did it by His word; that is, He spoke and it happened. "Let there be light" and Bingo! there was light. "Let there be plants and oceans and mountains. Let there be creatures that walk on the land and creatures that swim in the ocean and creatures that fly in the air and creatures that swing from the trees by their tails and creatures that crawl up out of the bathtub drain." The image is not of some somber God with a blueprint and a clipboard, but of an energetic elf dancing through the universe delighted with His creation and His own creativity. "And God saw everything that he had made, and behold, it was very good" (Gen. 1:31). God saw at the very beginning that the Creation was good, and He hasn't changed His mind.

The image changes in the creation of humankind. Now we see this God, who simply spoke worlds into being, hovering over a pile of dirt and breathing into it the breath of life. Humankind was a different creation because God would impart some of His own attributes and powers to this creature: the ability to plan or to plot, to know the difference between right and wrong, to create or destroy. We are a supercreature, you see, able to build tall buildings in a single bound, able to invent powerful locomotives and speeding bullets. We came to earth with powers and abilities far beyond those of other creatures. And we are disguised as mild-mannered reporters, truck drivers, dentists, and teachers. But beneath that suit, we wear another suit with a big S on the front, a bundle of explosive power with potential for great creativity or destruction. To be childlike is to be forever searching for a phone booth.

Creativity often appears dressed in the guise of mischief. In the controlling of the mischief we risk stifling the creativity. When I was in the second grade, we moved to a new school. It was the first time I had ever seen acoustic ceiling tile (those twelve-inch square tiles with little holes in them). A kid in my class figured that if you held your pencil down beside the inkwell and launched it with a rubber band, sometimes it would stick in one of those holes. The rest of us caught on quickly and kept our pencils sharpened just in case the teacher would leave the room, thus presenting us with our opportunity. Once, when the teacher came back, she was greeted by the sight of a couple dozen pencils hanging in the ceiling. She interpreted that behavior as disruptive, destructive mischief, and punished anyone who wasn't still holding his or her pencil. In programming out the mischief, she risked stifling the creativity. That pencil, you see, was an Atlas rocket, that inkwell was a launching pad, and that spot in the ceiling was the most distant star to which no one had ever shot a rocket before. Creativity presents itself in all sorts of disguises in adults as well. Look for it and encourage it.

Spontaneity. You know what spontaneity is when you wake up at 3 A.M. starving for a pizza and then actually get up and go get one. It's a childlike trait that shouldn't be lost, even though as a responsible adult you must honor schedules and deadlines. *Deadlines:* one of the ugliest words in the English language. "Dead" is the end and "line" is a boundary. Childlikeness doesn't care much for boundaries or death. It gives itself permission to climb over fences, to wade through a puddle in your best shoes, to say hello to a stranger in an elevator, to go roller-skating instead of going to the theater.

Jesus honored that spontaneous trait in people. When He called His disciples, He simply said, "Come with me and I will make you fishers of men" and they dropped their fishnets and followed. The terms of His approach triggered something like childlikeness in them.

By the way, when you wake up at 3 A.M. craving a pizza and wanting company, too, be sure you call someone who appreciates childlike spontaneity.

Trust. In our society, trust is not only not highly prized, it is seen as foolish and outdated. People who trust get ripped off and taken advantage of. "Buyer beware . . ." "Get it in writing . . ." Your associates won't be sympathetic: "Fool, why don't you grow up?" I have a friend who told me that he suspected that Ralph Nader worked for General Motors. You see, every time Nader forces the auto manufacturers to add more safety features to a car, it is the consumer who pays for it and GM makes more money. So he theorized that Nader was on the payroll to take the heat for the price increases. Interesting theory. I said to my friend, "What kind of person do I become if I go looking for the ulterior motive in people; if I always ask myself what does he mean by that, or what does he really want?"

It's better to be trusting and be thought naive than to be suspicious and spend one's whole life uncovering plots that never existed. Will Rogers said, "I would rather be the person who bought the Brooklyn Bridge than the one who sold it." All of that distrust becomes a lifestyle of its own after a while. Not only can you not trust anyone else, but you can no longer be trusted either. How we feel about other people is how we feel about ourselves. The faults we see in others are obvious to us because they are just like our own.

Children trust instinctively. When you were little, did you have any fear that your dad would drop you when he tossed you in the air? No, you trusted completely. My dad told me a riddle once. If you are outside a house that has no windows and no doors, how do you get in? Answer: you run around and around the house *until you are all in*. I ran around and around the house until I was exhausted. I didn't know the definition of riddle, joke, or play on words, but I knew the definition of trust. Even after it hadn't worked, I didn't question my father's trustworthiness. I just assumed that I hadn't run long enough.

I trusted what I saw on television. I would watch "Superman" and then go outside with a towel tied around my shoulders and jump off the front porch rail.

It didn't bother me that our house had a chimney that went straight from the roof to the furnace with no fireplace in between. I figured Santa Claus would solve that problem. Sure enough, on Christmas morning, the cookies and milk were gone and the presents were under the tree. I couldn't explain it, but I trusted it.

It didn't bother me when I learned in first-grade science that rabbits don't lay eggs. I still went to Easter egg hunts with great expectations and came home with my basket full of Easter eggs.

Can we relearn trust? Can we take what others say at face value until they give us reason to do otherwise? Can we trust the world and let some of the mysteries of life remain just that, mysteries? Some things are better left unexplained and undefined. Jesus said that the childlike were blessed for "to such belongs the kingdom of heaven" (Matt. 19:14). That means the kingdom can only be perceived through childlike eyes. It is never found through rational thinking and scientific method; it is found in trust and creativity. Only the childlike can really hear the words of Jesus when He said, "Do not be anxious about your life, what you shall eat or what you shall drink, nor about your body, what you shall put on. . . . Look at the birds of the air; they neither sow nor reap nor gather into barns, and yet your heavenly Father feeds them. Are you not of more value than they? . . . Consider the lilies of the field, how they grow; they neither toil nor spin; yet I tell you, even Solomon in all his glory was not arrayed like one of these" (Matt. 6:25–29). This is not practical advice. If you take it literally, you will starve, that is, if you don't die of exposure first. It's the language of the spirit, of the Kingdom, of childlike trust.

Joy. Enjoying little things is perhaps the most obvious and easily illustrated of the childlike attributes. Did you ever get a child a $39.95 batteries-not-included mechanical wonder for a Christmas gift? Remember how he tossed it aside and played with the box? That toy only does what it was designed to do; the box is anything your imagination will let it be: a house, a cave, the bridge of the Starship *Enterprise.*

A bumper sticker reads, "You can tell the men from the boys by the cost of their toys." Adults tend to get larger and more expensive mechanical devices. I think adults ought to get larger boxes, perhaps a refrigerator crate. Set aside a few minutes a day to get in there and play. Take a magic marker and draw gauges and dials and be Buck Rogers for a few minutes.

When I was a kid, one of my favorite toys was a coffee can lid. In those days, coffee cans were flatter and larger in diameter. There was a key on the bottom with which you unwound the lid. It was the prototype for the frisbee. A metal frisbee with a sharp edge posed some risk, but I spent hours sailing it over the top of our house where it would catch the afternoon breeze and come sailing back. What a joy! How inexpensive. The fact that my parents were caffeine addicts meant that I would get a new one every few days to replace the ones that collected on our roof. Children don't know what things cost, they only know what things are worth.

I used to delight in the discovery of a four-leaf clover or a jar of lightning bugs or watching my white mice have babies. Now that I'm an adult, I hire a gardener, an exterminator, and a veterinarian.

My first car cost $50, and I nearly waxed the paint off it. I would stand for hours admiring its sleek lines, its glowing paint, the futuristic look of its fender skirts and twin antennas with matching fox tails. It was a beauty, accented by flipper hub caps and a pair of sponge-rubber dice hanging from the mirror. I would study it from every angle and in every light. Oh, how I took joy in that car. My newest car cost $12,000 and I had it teflon coated so I wouldn't have to fool around with waxing it. For what have I traded my childlikeness?

Humility. Augustine said, "Should you ask me: what is the first thing in religion? I should reply: the first, second and third thing therein is humility." The *Encyclopedia of Religious Quotations* records: "True humility is but a right estimate of ourselves as God sees us." That's also a good definition of childlikeness—to see ourselves as God sees us.

The essence of childlikeness is caught up in this fairy tale I heard when I was a child. It was about a princess whose father wanted to get her a gift. He, being the king, could get her anything her heart desired. So, one night he asked her what she would like more than anything else in the world. She asked for the moon. He made the mistake that adults in power often make, he consulted with his advisers who did a feasibility study and an environmental impact report. They told the king that the gift was impossible to acquire and they told him why. They told him how big it was, how heavy it was, and how far away it was. Sadly, the king went to his daughter's room and told her that he couldn't get the gift that she wanted more than anything in the world. And he told her why: he told her how big it was, how heavy it was, and how far away it was. She said, "No it's not. It's about the same size as my thumb because when I hold my thumb up and squint one eye it covers the whole thing. And it's not that far away; it gets tangled up in the branches outside my window every evening." That's a childlike perception and there are times when it is the best perception.

I have always been a fan of the Muppets. My friends know that. So when the first Muppet movie was released, they were eager to report to me that while Kermit rides a bicycle in the movie, you can see the wires and strings. Not yet having seen the movie, I declared that they were wrong. Why? Because I know that Kermit can ride a bicycle without the aid of wires and strings. I choose to perceive it that way.

Some people go through life looking for wires and strings. How sad. Some people think rainbows are light refraction on water vapor condensed in the air. How dull. Some people think rainbows are God's promise to His children. I cast my lot with the latter group, not just because they are probably more fun, but because people who take joy in the lilies of the field and the birds of the air, who can see the hand of God in a rainbow and cover the moon with their thumb can't be far from the kingdom of God.

In conclusion, let me underscore with emphasis the declaration I made at the beginning of the chapter. There is a distinct difference between childlikeness and childishness. No one ever accuses a truly childlike person of not acting his age. The same cannot be said of the childish.

Some say that people become more childlike as they become elderly, but what they are often referring to is moodiness, forgetfulness, and bed-wetting. To be childlike is not a function of diminished brain activity but a conscious choice made to enrich life no matter what our position on the age continuum might be. Indeed to be truly childlike, one must acknowledge where he or she is on the continuum and be comfortable with that position. Children never try to hide their age. They are proud of it and eager to tell it. That's why the second question we ask children after asking their name is "How old are you?" They are delighted to give you that information, they will usually give it in precise detail, not only in years, but in fractions of years.

Someone once said, "Man is the only animal who plants grass in the spring and fights its growth all summer." We are also the only animal that fights its age all through life. All of the jokes and quips I know about aging are negative, except the quote from Albert Camus who said, "To grow old is to pass from passion to compassion." When you think about it, all the words we use to describe our age positions are negative words. We say to one another, "Don't be so infantile or juvenile or adolescent." Even the word *mature* sounds like *manure*. The most colorless phase of all is *middle age*. It's that time when we should be at the top of our game. It's the best part of life most will say, yet we identify it with those drab words, "middle age." It has been said that middle age is that time when you are warned to slow down by a doctor rather than a policeman.

When I was in seminary, the program was a three-year course. They called the first year the "junior year" because they didn't want to subject us to the indignity of being freshman yet another time. The last year was called, of course, the "senior year." The middle year was called, you guessed it, the "middle year." It wasn't the beginning or the end, just the middle. Students passing through that year of school were called "middlers." What could be more awful?

Perhaps that's the reason why people don't like to admit that they are entering middle age, because the name we gave it is so distasteful. Of course none of these terms is so repugnant or as starkly brutal as the word *old*. No one wants to be called "old," so we soften it by changing it to *older* or use euphemisms like *senior citizen*.

Let us embrace our age with joy and expectation. Each stage of life offers its own challenges and adventures. We should be happy to move into the next room of our life, to play with the new furniture and explore the secret places, to taste it all with childlike delight. Just once I would like to hear someone say when asked their age, "I'm forty-five and three-quarters."

I would like to recommend that we abandon the terminology we use to talk about age. If we change the way we talk about it, it may change the way we think about it. Let's loose all those bland and demeaning words and acknowledge only three ages: *too young*, *too old*, and *the rest of us*. So take a look at yourself. If you're not too young or too old, you must be one of the rest of us.

I met a man once from an African tribe where they didn't record birth dates. So he not only didn't know when his birthday was, he didn't know how old he was. He smiled and asked, "If you didn't know how old you were, how old would you be?" There's a question that a childlike spirit can really get a hold of. He was a man who had that choice available to him everyday, and I suddenly realized so did I.

The childlike spirit loves choices, new adventures, secrets, and mysteries. Harry Emerson Fosdick, that great preacher of this century, said, "I would rather live in a world where my life is surrounded by mystery than live in a world so small that my mind would comprehend it." Fosdick was an old man when he said that, or perhaps he was just one of "the rest of us." The childlike spirits are those who know that childhood is not just a stage to be passed through as a training event in preparation for adult life. Childhood is a gift to be celebrated for what it is, and the wise among us will keep some of the good stuff of childhood and carry it with them their whole lives. Indeed the great people I know are those who have kept childhood's greatest gift, childlikeness, and have joined to it the wisdom that comes with years.

Fosdick may indeed be the perfect example of what I have been describing. He was one of the most respected preachers in America, pastor of one of its best-known churches, author of many books, a man with schedules and deadlines and responsibilities. By all measures he was a great and mature man. Yet in his writings about faith he displays his genuine childlike wisdom. In *The Meaning of Faith*, he wrote about air as formula and experience:

> If one inquires what air is, the answer will probably be a formula stating that oxygen and nitrogen mixed in proportions of 32 to 79 make air. But air in experience is not a formula. Air is the elixir we breathe and live thereby. Air is the magician who takes the words that our lips frame and bears them from friend to friend in a daily converse. Air is the messenger who carries music to our ears and fragrance to our nostrils; it is the whisper among the trees in June, and in March the wild dancer who shakes the bare branches for his castanets. Air is the giant who piles the surf against the rocky shore, and the nurse who fans the faces of the sick. One cannot put that into a formula.

I would be willing to bet that Fosdick was a man who, once in a while, between deadlines and scheduled appointments, squinted one eye and covered the moon with his thumb.

I conclude with a description actress Glenn Close wrote about her daughter. In it she captures some of the essence of childlikeness:

> Our daughter is one year old. She is a brilliant actor because she lives absolutely and truthfully moment to moment. She's not interested in the movie that may or may not be made. She could care less about the deal that may or may not fall through or the part that may or may not be offered. She is interested in lunch, a beautiful flower, a tiny speck on the rug, the wind in high branches, a bird flying across the setting sun. She has taught me that after all the compulsion and ambition, and anxiety, the little moments are the sum of our lives, not the huge, earth-shattering events. Life is now.

Jesus said, "Let the children come to me, and do not hinder them; for to such belongs the kingdom of God. Truly, I say to you, whoever does not receive the kingdom of God like a child shall not enter it" (Luke 18:16–17).

A child was busy at work with a pencil and pad. An adult asked what he was doing. He replied, "I'm drawing a picture of God." "Oh," exclaimed the adult. "But no one knows what God looks like." The child responded confidently, "They will when I'm finished."

Perhaps childlike creativity is always the doorway through which revelation enters.

- Let your childlikeness shine through.
- When creative, spontaneous, even silly impulses come, don't stifle them, celebrate them.

12

Sidetracks

I bumped into an old friend whom I hadn't seen in a long time. She asked how I was doing. It wasn't just one of those casual how-are-you-doing greetings, but a sincere inquiry into my well-being in the time that had elapsed since we last spoke. So I gave her the rundown on what had been happening in my life, what had gone well and what hadn't, what I planned to do more of, and what I planned to phase out. After about ten minutes of mono-logue, I paused, and she said, "Yes, but are you happy?" For her that was the ultimate barometer by which the quality of life was measured. That's true of most of us.

How many times have you heard someone say, "It's all right as long as it makes you happy." Happiness for most of us is the primary quest. People write best-selling books about how to achieve it. Thoughtful people contemplate the key to happiness with the same intensity and devotion as the holy men of old contemplated the meaning of life. It's even written into one of the cornerstones of our nation, the Declaration of Independence: "We hold these Truths to be self-evident, that all Men are created equal, that they are endowed by their Creator with certain un-alienable Rights, that among these are Life, Liberty, and the Pur-suit of Happiness."

We probably take "the Pursuit of Happiness" more seriously

than any other phrase in any public document ever written. We run our little legs down to stumps pursuing happiness. Don't misunderstand me; I'm in favor of happiness for myself and for everyone else. It's just that happiness is not found in the pursuit thereof. Happiness is a fringe benefit. Happiness is a by-product. It is a gift given to those found in proper pursuits. Don't be side-tracked running after happiness. Work rather for kindness, gentleness of spirit, generosity, and love, and happiness will come. It's like the butterfly that you chase and chase that is always just beyond the reach of your net. Exhausted, you sit to rest, and the butterfly comes and lands on your shoulder.

Security is not a worthy quest either, because it doesn't really exist. It's an illusion, a will-o'-the-wisp. That's why we tend to refer to it as a sense of security. You may achieve a sense of it, but you won't achieve it.

When I was traveling around in my van doing concerts and seminars—sort of a troubadour-style hand-to-mouth existence—I would have to get paid in cash so I could put gas in the van for the next stop on my tour. A friend in Detroit marveled that I could live with that kind of insecurity. He was an electronics whiz and worked for Ford doing computer designing for car parts. Lots of money equals lots of security. The next year when I returned, he had been fired and was having trouble finding another job because his salary was so high and his field so specialized. I, on the other hand, had a new job about three times a week. Who had the security? Neither of us. He had a sense of security for a while.

The real tragedy is that in order to create and maintain that illusion of security, we have to design a life around predictability with as little change as possible. Thus we trade some of the best things in life—adventure, growth, surprise, spontaneity—for a ghost, a myth called security.

In *Will You Be My Friend?* James Kavanaugh wrote, "There is no security. Security is sameness and fear, the postponing of life. Security is expectations and commitments and premature death." Security is the stifler of life, while risk is what adds zest to life. Why do so many old men talk with such glee about their experiences in World War II, even tragic experiences. There was a day-to-day or hour-to-hour quality about their lives; they were in a business with inherent risk: people were shooting at them. There was an immediacy about life that energized them. If you didn't expect to see the sun rise tomorrow, you might pay more attention to the sunset tonight. So rather than trying to build more security into your life, try to build in more risk. D. H. Lawrence said, "The essence of spirit is to choose the thing which did not better one's position, but made it more perilous."

My friend, Karen Wetther, wrote this poem. It might help you to know that she has managed a successful career in spite of severe crippling arthritis.

> To laugh
> is to risk appearing the fool,
> To cry
> is to risk appearing sentimental,
> To reach out for another is to
> risk involvement—
> To expose feelings is to risk
> exposing your true self—
> To place your ideas, your dreams
> before the crowd is to risk loss—
> To love is to risk not being
> loved in return—
> To live is to risk dying
> To hope is to risk despair—
> To try at all is to risk failure—
> But to risk we must . . .
> because the greatest hazard in life
> is to risk nothing.
> The man, the woman who risks
> nothing . . .
> does nothing, has nothing,
> is nothing.

Happiness and *security*: lovely greeting-card words that we wish for all our friends and loved ones and ourselves. They are hemlock. Their pursuit is a dead end for the spirit. Don't chase them. Let them surprise you by coming to dwell in your house from time to time, never as a permanent member of the family, but as an old friend who just stopped by for a while to say hello and make you smile.

Lest you assume that I have added *happiness* and *security* to my list of negative terms, let me reiterate that they are not, but the quest for them is a sidetrack.

One of the most often misquoted statements in the Bible is that "money is the root of all evil." Actually the phrase reads, "The love of money is the root of all evils" (1 Tim. 6:10). In the following verse Paul used the word *craving*. Money is not bad or harmful, it is the craving after it that is a sidetrack. So with happiness and security, it is the craving for them that leads us off the path.

If we are Christians, our quest, our craving is to be found faithful to the call of Christ in our lives, to be doing the work and the will of God. Let your happiness be the joy that is a gift to those who are found pleasing to God and employed in the work of His kingdom. Let your security be the security that comes from knowing that your name is written in the Book of Life.

Only when the quest for happiness and security is abandoned for nobler guests can we get on with the mystery and the joy and learn the surprising lessons of life. Those learnings will come with the passing of time as surely as the dawn will come after the darkness. Let us not be sidetracked somewhere in the underbrush, but rather place ourselves in an ideal vantage point for observing and celebrating the dawn when it does come.

> After a while you learn the subtle difference
> Between holding a hand and chaining a soul,
> And you learn that love doesn't mean leaning
> And company doesn't mean security,
> And you begin to learn that kisses aren't contracts
> And presents aren't promises,
> And you begin to accept your defeats
> With your head up and your eyes open,
> And learn to build all your roads
> On today because tomorrow's ground
> Is too uncertain for plans and futures
> Have a way of falling down in mid-flight.

After a while you learn that even sunshine
Burns if you get too much.
So you plant your own garden and decorate
Your own soul, instead of waiting
For someone to bring you flowers
And you learn that you really can endure . . .
That you really are strong
And you really do have worth.
And you learn and learn . . .
With every goodbye you learn.

Happiness and security are not goals, they are gifts. Examine the goals of your life. Set worthwhile, difficult, even threatening ones. Struggle toward them. Notice how the resulting exhilaration of having risked and survived brings with it some companions: security and happiness.

13

The Source

The story is told of T. E. Lawrence's (better known as Lawrence of Arabia) bringing several Arab leaders to the Versailles Peace Conference so that their interests would be considered in the making of the peace following the First World War. These desert people were awestruck by the sights of Paris, but nothing so astonished them as did the water taps in their hotel rooms. To them, water was such a luxury, and here in their rooms it was free and seemed to be without end. All one had to do was turn the tap.

At the conclusion of the conference, when time came for them to return to the desert, these Arabs went about removing the faucets. They believed they had found magical wells which would provide their people with all the water they needed. They didn't understand that the faucets would only function when connected to a water supply.

Just as most people innately know that part of who we are is spirit, we also sense that there is a spirit outside ourselves. It is a great spirit that sort of flows through everything and binds everything together. Religion calls it God, the Source of our being. Philosophy calls it the Prime Mover, who remaining unmoved moves all. The guy who fixes my car calls it the Man Upstairs. And Obi-Wan Kenobi called it the Force. Some people don't call it anything, but they suspect that it is there.

That spirit and your spirit are of the same substance, and it is that spirit that energizes and renews yours. So it is important to find a way to get connected to that source. Many people find that connectedness in religion and others find it in meditation or by being close to nature. Some say that music, art, poetry, and other creative endeavors are ways to get plugged into it. It is certain, however, that our spirits can dry up unless our faucet is connected to *the* Source.

In these next pages I want to say some things about the quest for that Source—some things about what makes the quest difficult, about our attitudes and perceptions that tend to sabotage our own efforts, and, I hope, some things that will encourage you to take up the quest again if you have currently abandoned it, to look with new eyes and search in previously unexplored places.

Although we are created in the image of God by the hand of God, we are not gods. We are part of the creation. We therefore exist within boundaries of time and space and cannot reach beyond those parameters. Do you remember the first time you tried to get your mind around the concept of endless space? Endlessness is not a concept for which we have a program in our computer banks. Our minds don't work outside the concept of spatial relationships. Nonetheless we try to visualize the end of space. You get into your spacesuit, board your rocket, and travel for a billion light-years or so and finally come to a wall. That's it, the end of space. But that's not it. Your finite mind knows that there is more space on the other side. It's frustrating!

A few years later in a science class you see diagrams and drawings of the smallest particles in the universe, the so-called building blocks of matter, the atoms, and you realize that they look like miniature solar systems. What if they are solar systems? What if our solar system is really an atom and the earth is really an electron spinning around a nucleus in the handle of some gigantic frying pan somewhere?

Later you come across those theories that assert that the universe actually turns in on itself, which means that if you could travel at the speed of light for an infinite amount of time you would ultimately not get to the edge of infinity (the wall), but rather back to where you started. It all sounds like the script of a "Star Trek" episode. If I think about that stuff for too long, I get a headache. My mind is not set up in such a way that it can deal with that kind of information. I am not programmed for this, this is the stuff that God thinks about!

God doesn't have my limitations. God exists outside of time and space, outside of creation. I use the word "outside" not in any geographical sense, for God is everywhere, but in the sense that God is a kind of reality beyond our comprehension, our understanding, or our knowing. God exists in an eternal, unlimited reality, unknowable with the equipment we have available to us. He is infinite, eternal; we are finite, created beings. The two don't interact. We can't even talk about God because, as Paul Tillich and other theologians have pointed out, to attach any descriptive terms at all to God is to limit Him. If I say God is great, it precludes the possibility that God is small. If I say God is strong, I have said that God cannot be weak. If I say God is good, I preclude from His character the possibility of His being the source of evil. Indeed, in my use of personal pronouns I have described God as male and ignored the possibility of female traits in His character. God is above description, above the capacity of my language to define Him. All I can safely say about God is "God is." Anything beyond that is limiting and therefore contrary to the nature of an all-powerful God. Perhaps that's why when God introduced Himself to Moses on the mountain in the story referred to earlier, He simply said, "I Am."

About Maleness and Femaleness. Philosophy asserts that the creator cannot be less than the creation. That means that God must be understood as embodying everything that it means to be male and everything it means to be female and infinitely more. Our Scriptures hint at this truth. The Bible was written in a highly patriarchal society, so it follows that God would be characterized as male. Men in that society were the only ones with rights, power, or freedom. It wouldn't make sense to refer to God in any other way. Yet, all through the Bible, there are images of God displaying characteristics that can only be described as feminine. In the Torah (Deut. 32:11), God is characterized as an eagle, a strong enough masculine image, but the eagle "flutters over its young, spreading out its wings, catching them." It is the teaching, nurturing function of the mother eagle that is being described. Isaiah says that God "goes forth like a mighty man, . . . he shows himself mighty against his foes" (Isa. 42:13). In the very next verse, however, it says, "I will cry out like a woman in travail" (Isa. 42:14). Why the mixed metaphor? Perhaps neither metaphor is adequate in itself, so you say everything you have and still come up short in the task of defining the undefinable.

Jesus chose the same feminine imagery, by the way, in John 16:21. It's one of the most poignant scenes anywhere in literature. Jesus is outside the walls of Jerusalem, that city that He came to save, that city that refused to welcome Him. His heart is breaking with love and compassion over this city of God that has lost her way. He laments, "O Jerusalem, Jerusalem, killing the prophets and stoning those who are sent to you! How often would I have gathered your children together as a hen gathers her brood under her wings, and you would not!" (Luke 13:34).

Here Jesus doesn't even compare Himself to an eagle, but to a hen, not a very masculine image at all. At that moment, however, the most appropriate image He could call on was that of a mother hen trying to protect her brood under her outstretched wings. But, in this instance, the brood refused to come to the protective shelter.

Growing up in Kansas and spending some time on a farm, I've observed that scene played out in the barnyard: the mother hen with all her chicks following after her, picking at the ground, clucking and chirping. Then some imminent danger invades their tranquility—a dog, an airplane, a kid with a slingshot—and all the chicks scurry under those big, welcoming outstretched wings. You can't imagine that they all could fit, but they do; not one is missing or left out. When my little finite brain tries to comprehend how God could care for everyone in the world and hear all our prayers at the same time and be present to all of us everywhere at once, I remember the image of the mother hen and am assured that God is God and no one is missing.

I referred earlier in this book to the fact that the most popular image among Christians used to describe the transformation that takes place when our spirit is reunited with the spirit of our

Creator is that of new birth. Jesus said to Nicodemus in John 3:3 that he needed to be "born anew." Giving new birth to our spirit is the greatest gift that God has to offer us. It is the fondest hope and desire of all devout seekers after God, that they might receive the gift of new birth. Giving birth is a *female* function! The greatest gift that God has to offer to us created mortals, God offers as a mother.

If we are going to attempt the task of defining the undefinable, we must use all the tools, metaphors, and images at hand. Even then it won't be enough. Virginia Ramey Mollenkott observed in an article published in the *Circuit Rider*: "Perhaps one reason our culture has strayed so far from a dynamic sense of God's presence within us is that our Judeo-Christian tradition has ignored or suppressed the feminine images of God, the very images that most strongly imply imminence, nearness, intimacy and involvement."

Having said that, let me acknowledge that I will from time to time in this writing continue to refer to God as *He*. That not only betrays the fact that I am a product of my culture, but it also points out the inadequacy of our language. We have no good pronouns that mean both male and female or are above sexuality. We can't refer to God as "It" because that term lacks the sense of personalness described in the above quote. So whenever you see the word *He*, make a mental reference to this explanation and understand my meaning.

A Glimpse at Best

So all of this conversation serves to illustrate that any understanding of God must begin with the acknowledgment that we are embarking on an impossible task. We live in a different world, a created world of time and space. His world is beyond our comprehension. The word *eternity* is in our dictionaries, but we can't really define it because any definition we might concoct would necessarily include a concept of time. We would say, "Eternity is a long time or an endless period of time." No! Eternity is the absence of time! I have been asked by people, "How long is eternity?" That is a nonsense question. Eternity is not a time or a place but a state of being wherein time and space are not applicable concepts. Eternity is the state of being in which God exists, and we can't go there, at least not in our mortal state.

If there is a wall in the universe it stands between time and eternity, Creation and Creator, finite and infinite. We cannot transverse the barrier, but God can. We do not go to God; He comes to us. He comes to us in forms that our finite minds can grasp. He comes to us as father, mother, friend, beauty, peace, love, and truth.

We cannot find the truth; truth finds us. God is not discovered by us. He is revealed to us by Himself. The ancient Hebrews believed that if they saw God, they would die. No doubt correct in that we can only see God if we exist on the same plane as He does. In order to do that, we have to give up mortal being, thus die. In Exod. 33:23, it is said that God gave Moses a view of His back as He passed by. The point is this, since God is the only one who can pass through the dividing wall into our limited world and since God can only be interpreted through our limited concepts and understandings, it follows that what we can know about God is precious little. The best we can ever hope for is a glimpse of Him as He passes by, not a full frontal view. We can know only what our little computer systems are programmed to handle, only what God the master programmer chooses to reveal. Moses only got a look at His back, and that's the best look anyone has had since.

Thus I tend to greet with consternation (mixed with mirth), those people who insist that they have God all figured out. They can summarize everything you need to know about God in three easy lessons, and they are eager to do so. They speak with glib confidence as if God were a toad they had just dissected in their laboratory and now they have complete knowledge of truth. They now see themselves as conquerors of God and behave accordingly. Whoever first said that "a little truth is dangerous" was certainly right. In *The Meaning of Faith*, Harry Emerson Fosdick said, "Those who define him best understand him least."

All we can ever hope for is the faintest glimpse of truth, and, if we are granted that glimpse, it should produce in us humility, not arrogance. My source for this understanding is Isaiah, one of the great prophets of the Old Testament and the one whose writings Jesus quoted more than any other. Isaiah was granted a vision of

God, "sitting upon a throne, high and lifted up; and his train filled the temple" (Isa. 6:1). Isaiah's response to this glorious vision of a king surrounded by chanting angels was to say, "Woe is me! For I am lost!" (Isa. 6:5). It's a good test of the authenticity of one's glimpse of truth: does the bearer of that word of truth carry it humbly, as if it were a priceless treasure and he an unworthy vessel, or as if it were a trophy that he has won? Does the bearer of that witness say, "Look at me, I found it!" or "Woe is me, I am lost and it has found me"? One who has truly been granted a glimpse of truth will never assume he has the whole truth, but will search joyfully for others who may also have been given a glimpse. Then they eagerly compare their pieces of the puzzle to see if they fit and if together they reveal a larger part of the whole.

The fable of the blind men and the elephant is appropriate here. You all know how it goes: the men, being blind, had to experience the elephant with their sense of touch. One felt the tail and said an elephant is like a snake, the next felt the side and said the elephant is like a wall, the third man felt his leg and said the elephant is like a tree, and so on. If only they had pooled their information, they might have been able to construct an image of what an elephant was really like.

It is no accident that the New Testament uses physical blindness as a metaphor for a corresponding spiritual condition. Nor is it an accident that the most common miracle stories in the New Testament are about blind people receiving their sight. I find it significant that Jesus' methods varied from case to case. In one story, He touched the blind man's eyes, and he was healed. In a second story, Jesus simply spoke to the blind man, and he was healed. In a third story, He spit on the ground, made little mudpacks, applied them to a man's eyes, and then instructed him to go to the river and wash them off. The man eagerly complied and, with the washing completed, discovered that he could see.

That's where the story ends, but if you will allow a little imaginative speculation, perhaps we can create a new fable of our own about three blind men who experience, not an elephant, but the works of God. In our fable these three former blind men, all having been healed of their blindness, happen to meet. They probably meet at the video store, but that's irrelevant.

As people who have had miraculous experiences are apt to do, they begin to share. The first man says, "I used to be blind, but Jesus healed me." The second responds, "The exact same thing happened to me." The third chimes in, "Well, isn't it a small world!" Then they begin to analyze their experiences more closely.

The first man says, "I know how He does it. When He reaches out to touch your eyes, a power surge fuses your optic nerve." The second man says, "What are you talking about? Jesus doesn't touch your eyes; He just speaks. He says the magic words 'Be Healed,' and that's when it happens." The first man retorts, "Yes, He does say the magic words, but He has to be touching your eyes when He says them." The second answers, "Jesus isn't into touchy feely stuff; He just speaks." The first says, "Well, I was there, so I ought to know!" Finally the third man adds, "You guys have both got it wrong. What He really does is spit on the ground, make little mud pies, and put the goo on your eyes." The other two glower back, "That's disgusting! Jesus would never do that! He just touches you with a clean hand!" "No!" says the second man, "He just speaks! No touching! No spitting!"

So they all go off in separate directions and form their own churches. The first man's church holds hands and hugs a lot. The second man's church is into the spoken word and the power of verbosity. I'm afraid to go to the third man's church, the Church of the Mud Spitters. I think the sacraments could be a little weird.

There is a moral to this rather absurd little fable: all three of these men were *still* blind. If they had really received their sight and glimpsed the divine, they would have been so busy celebrating that fact, particularly with others who had also been healed, they wouldn't have time to argue process. Perhaps that's why so many churches these days spend so much of their time and energy arguing process, that's all they have to talk about. They are too blind to stand in awe before the miracle.

I am suggesting that the reason so much of our society seems irreligious is not because they have rejected God, but they have rejected the image of God presented to them by their parents, their traditions, and their religious institutions. A recent survey showed that more than 70 percent of Americans believe that there is a God, but only a fraction of that number participate in any religious organization or church. They haven't rejected God; they have rejected that teeny-weeny, narrow-minded, irrelevant god offered to them. We need a God who is bigger than us. We have outgrown the god of the church and don't know how to seek the God of the Universe.

J. B. Phillips in his marvelous little book, now old but still relevant, *Your God Is Too Small*, writes, "Let us fling wide the doors and windows of our minds and make some attempt to appreciate the 'size' of God. He must not be limited to religious matters or even to the 'religious' interpretation of life. He must not be confined to one particular section of time or must one imagine Him as the local God of this planet or even only of the universe that astronomical survey has so far discovered."

Phillips suggested that the god the world has outgrown and given up on is not God at all, but some weak representation of God designed by someone who at one time may have had a pinhole glimpse of truth. He also suggests that it may be necessary to put our little god to rest before we can begin the mysterious adventure of discovering or, more correctly, being discovered by the real God.

The Conduct Conspiracy

I outgrew my god for the first time when I was six years old. It was about the same time I figured out that Santa Claus was a fraud. It just came to me one day when I was walking home from the first grade, the whole thing was a setup contrived by adults to control my conduct: "You'd better watch out, you'd better not cry, you'd better not pout, I'm telling you why, Santa Claus is coming to town. He sees you when you're sleeping; he knows when you're awake; he knows when you've been bad or good, so be good for goodness sake."

My mother used to remind me of Santa's omnipresence when it came my turn to dry the dishes. Not having any sisters, my brother and I had to alternate on the domestic chores. When the debate would erupt about who did it last, my mother would inject the Santa-is-watching warning, which had special power in the weeks just before Christmas.

On that day of discovery, I kicked myself all the way home from school. All those years (six!) I had fallen for a story designed only to get me to modify my behavior. What a dummy I was! I can still remember the look on my mother's face when I got home and broke the news in a rather abrupt confrontation.

She was doing the laundry (she called it "the washing" [spelled with an r]). She did the laundry a lot in those days, and the sights, sounds, and smells associated with the process are still vivid to me. I remember how angry she would get when the clothes wrapped around the wringer of the washing machine. I remember the sound the machine made as she swung the wringer over the tub that held the rinse water, and it snapped into place. I remember how the house smelled on wash days. Mom used kerosene to help get the grease out of Dad's work clothes, and that, combined with the bleach, produced vapors that wafted in the air and linger in my memory still. Sometimes she would serve a lunch of navy beans and ham with fried potatoes. It was my favorite. Dad didn't like fried potatoes, so Mom and I would have them for lunch. It was our special treat, our secret. I loved the smell of navy beans and bleach and kerosene, and I loved my mother for all that work she did.

That's why I still remember her hurt expression as I looked her square in the face and said, "There isn't really a Santa Claus is there?" It was as if I had hit her with a brick. A second passed that could have been a year, and she said simply, "No." I could only realize in retrospect the extent to which that moment hurt her. I would take back the moment if I could. But what for her was a moment of sadness, was for me a moment of liberation. I was free from the fat old man with cheeks so rosy and a smile so merry, who surfaces once a year to give gifts to the children of parents who can afford them and the rest of the year exists only as a threat. But as they say, with freedom comes responsibility, the new awareness represented a corresponding loss of innocence and the joy inherent in it.

In that little moment before my mother answered my life-changing question, we both watched the ghosts of Christmas Past parade across the laundry room. There was the fun of decorating the tree together (Dad always did the lights), the joy of anticipating what was in the packages Santa had left, the excitement of trying to go to sleep knowing that the big event was only hours away. What fun they must have had getting everything ready while we slept.

I remember watching my dad cut something out of the paper, which in later years, reflecting back, I now identify as the stencil for my name, which appeared on the back of my red wagon found one year under the Christmas tree. How could my mom have kept from laughing as she helped me compose all of those notes to Santa Claus left with the milk and cookies, knowing all the time that my dad would be the one to finish the snacks, leaving the empty glass and some crumbs as evidence that Santa had sure enough been there? What incomparable joy it had been, but now it was over. Santa was gone now, along with my innocence, and I was alone with my responsibility.

I suppose the reason I outgrew God and Santa Claus at the same time is that they both appeared to me as the same person. At least the god that had been presented to me was the image of the Santa I had just rejected: a benevolent old grandfather type, flowing beard and all. He is always keeping track of your behavior to decide if you are worthy of all the gifts on Christmas Day. God had a decided advantage, however, over Santa—He, being omnipresent, could look into everyone's windows at the same time and, unlike Christmas Day, you were never sure when Judgment Day would be, so you couldn't get passing marks by shaping up during the few weeks just before. Just as my parents had used Santa, the church was using God to regulate my behavior. They both had to go when I became a responsible person, and go they did.

Perhaps it is necessary to shake off those phony little gods before one can hope to be granted a glimpse of the God who exists beyond time and space and what we call reality. I believe that that is precisely where many people are on their spiritual journey; those folks who call themselves agnostics, atheists, and doubters; those pilgrims who don't call themselves anything but are faced with the certainty that what the traditional religious community has to sell is not for them.

They are in the process of shaking off those little gods, a necessary step to freeing oneself for the real mystical adventure, that of allowing ourselves to be discovered by the God of the Universe, the God of Eternity, the Unknowable One.

Mysticism

I have used the words *mystical* and *mysterious* to describe that journey toward the Source. I am comfortable with those words, though I realize many are not. They conjure up images of sitting cross-legged on some mountain top in Tibet, chanting a mantra for about forty years, hoping for enlightenment. Or they imagine a strange lady with a turban behind a beaded curtain, speaking with a strange Eastern European accent as she examines your palm.

A mystic is anyone who agrees that there are realities all about us that cannot be experienced through the five senses or described in normal scientific terms. Scott Peck says in *The Different Drum*, "Mystics acknowledge the enormity of the unknown, but rather than being frightened by it, they seek to penetrate even deeper into it that they may understand more—even with the realization that the more they understand, the greater the mystery will become."

I had lunch not long ago with a member of my church who told me of the deepest concern of his life, the environment. He talked for nearly an hour about his love for the creation and all the agencies and causes he worked with and supported in the struggle to preserve the environment and turn back the ravages of overuse, misuse, and greed. When we got back to the church, I think he began to realize that we hadn't talked anything at all about "religion." In order to be polite he felt that he needed to talk about my field as well. So, a little apologetically, he admitted that he didn't have any concept of what it meant to be directed by God's spirit, that he didn't have any understanding of "religious experience."

"I guess," he said, "I'm not a very mystical person." As I got out of the car, I poked my head back in the window and said, "In order to be an environmentalist, you have to be a mystic." That understanding that environmentalists have of the connectedness of all of life, that deep appreciation of beauty, that nature is more than just a feast for the eyes and somehow intimately related to our own being as persons, that caring for little creatures (even the useless ugly ones), the sense that the loss of any species is an eternal loss for us all, that life is an interwoven fabric, a giant tapestry, and that any diminishing of a part of that life diminishes all of us—that awareness is what drives the environmentalist, and it is entirely mystical.

We are, I believe, as part of our spiritual awakening, beginning to recover a reverence for the creation that is akin to the best of the American Indian legacy. The Indians could never understand how anyone could own the land; if anything, the land owned the people. You couldn't possess what was alive and part of the same fabric as your own being. You couldn't own the land, only live gratefully in harmony with it. Robert J. Conley wrote in a poem in *The Christian Science Monitor*, "When I go to the supermarket and buy some meat pre-cut and wrapped, how do I apologize to the spirit of the animal whose meat I eat and where shall I build my fires?"

Our loss of connectedness with the spirits of other creatures and the land is one of the surest signals that we have lost ourselves and any hope at a glimpse of God. So we consult little gods mostly from dim memories or, worse yet, from theological formulas. The golden calf is still among us, and we wonder at the fact that so few want to join us in our worship. The mystics, even the ones who call themselves by other names like environmentalists, know better.

On Interstate Highway 8, about a hundred miles east of San Diego, you come across some amazing rock formations: mountains of stones that look as though they have been piled on top of one another by a playful God for His and our enjoyment. Just when your back is getting tired and the radio stations from the coast are starting to fade and the drive is getting boring, God has provided a wonder to cheer you on your journey. Someone climbed up on one of those big beautiful boulders and, with a can of spray paint, scrawled across its face the words, "Jesus Saves." If you were Sherlock Holmes and you wanted to figure out who had written that slogan on the rock, there would be one group of people you could eliminate as suspects immediately—Christians! Christians have too much respect for the rock and the God who put it there to put paint on it, no matter how profound the message.

Christians know that the rock itself makes a clearer and more excellent statement of the divine than any message a mere mortal could write on it. No, the guilty party is one of those spiritual Neanderthals still following after one of those silly little gods long since exposed as irrelevant and outgrown by most of society. I recommend that those people confine their scribbling to the walls of public restrooms until they have some inkling of the meaning of the words they have written.

Scott Peck sums it up in *The Different Drum*: "Mysticism, a much maligned word, is not an easy one to define. It takes many forms. Yet through the ages, mystics of every shade of religious belief have spoken of unity, of an underlying connectedness between things; between men and women, between us and other creatures and even inanimate matter as well, a fitting together according to an ordinarily invisible fabric underlying the cosmos."

Mystical experiences are not taken very seriously in our society. If you speak of them too much, someone is likely to call for a Ghostbuster. Yet I believe that there are those times when God breaks through in surprising and unusual ways. If we are to be healthy, beautiful spirits we must embrace those momentary glimpses, those opportunities to get connected to the source.

One of the most amazing of those mystical experiences is described in the ninth chapter of the Gospel of Luke. The story goes like this: It was Jesus' practice from time to time to withdraw from the crowds for some personal reflection and prayer. He took with Him Peter, James, and John, the same trio He would take with Him in the Garden of Gethsemane. And, just like on that occasion, they all got sleepy, but in this case they didn't stay asleep but awoke to behold Jesus in what the Bible calls a transfigured state. His garments were pure white. There was an aura about Him, sort of a glow. Of course everyone knew what that meant, it meant he had been face to face with God. It was just like when Moses came down from the mountain after receiving the Ten Commandments from God. His face glowed so much that they had to put a bag over His head to keep from driving the other people crazy. People with a holy glow about them often annoy the average person on the street.

So there before their eyes was this vision. Jesus was glowing just like Moses had, but He wasn't alone. Standing there with Him were none other than Moses and Elijah—Moses the lawgiver and Elijah the dean of the prophets. The Law and the prophets—you've heard that phrase over and over in the Bible. Remember when Jesus was asked what was the greatest commandment? He said, "You shall love the Lord your God with all your heart, and with all your soul, and with all your mind. . . . You shall love your neighbor as yourself." Then he added, "On these two commandments depend all the law and the prophets" (Matt. 22:37–40). Moses and Elijah represented all the law and the prophets.

Well, Peter was just overwhelmed. He always knew that Jesus had greatness in Him, that He would some day change the world for the better, but this scene was too wonderful to be imagined. There they were casually chatting about world issues: Moses and Elijah, two of the greatest heroes of the Hebrew nation and, standing with them, their boy Jesus.

Peter, who had a propensity for speaking at inappropriate times and saying something stupid, behaved true to form. He said, "It's great to be here! Let's build three booths, one for each of you, and just relish this wonderful moment."

It was a Hebrew custom to build booths, or little tabernacles or shrines, where special epiphanies took place, to mark the spot as a holy spot. Of course the church does the same thing. The place where Jesus was born has a church built on it. The place where He was buried has a church built on it. His boyhood home in Nazareth, Mary and Martha's home, the place where He fed the five thousand and recited the Beatitudes are all church sites. Someone has correctly observed that everything that ever happened of significance in the Holy Land happened under a church. That's all Peter really wanted, to capture the moment, to memorialize it so it would never be lost, to preserve it in time, this glorious and unimaginable vision.

Then a cloud moved in and engulfed them all. Everyone knew what that meant too. The cloud was God's symbol throughout the Old Testament. It was a cloud that had moved before the Israelites to guide them into the Promised Land. Then that terrible, unmistakable voice spoke from the cloud. It was the voice of God who spoke in brief and certain terms, "This is my Son, listen to Him!" Then the cloud lifted and Moses and Elijah were gone.

It was a mystical experience of the highest order, given as a gift to Peter. I am sure it was Peter's gift and not that of the other two disciples because of the scene that took place just before it in Luke's Gospel. It's that famous story where Jesus asked His disciples who people said that He was, what was the gossip around the countryside? Then He asked who *they* said He was. It was Peter who blurted out that Jesus was the Christ. It was a faith affirmation, yet to read the story you are not at all convinced that Peter was all that convinced. There is a feeling in the text that Peter might have liked to take those words back, but they were irretrievable. Then came the Transfiguration, the mystical experience to confirm his faith affirmation. Peter had said of Jesus, "You are the Christ," then God said in symbol and voice, "You are right, He is greater that Elijah, greater than Moses, listen to Him."

Mystical experiences are gifts of God given to us to let us know when we are on the right track. I said in the first lines of this chapter that we exist within time-and-space boundaries and cannot reach beyond them. In a way we do reach beyond them: in dreams, visions, and mystical experiences. The restraints of time and space fall away for just a moment, and we glimpse the infinite. It's God's way of inviting us to move in for a closer look.

The quest for the Source is not an easy one. There are no easy formulas or well-traveled and well-lighted paths. Since we and God exist on different levels of being and live in different realities, our contacts are at best going to be momentary and uncertain. And yet there is a perfection about those moments out of time when there is spiritual connectedness. It's like traveling through a foreign, even dangerous and unfamiliar, landscape only to find you have arrived at your own front door. There is a certain déjà vu about those times where we meet as strangers and recognize an unexplainable familiarity, even a comfortableness like kindred spirits know. Someone has said that in each of us there exists a God-shaped vacuum, an empty space that only God can fill. Augustine said that the soul cannot rest until it finds its rest in its creator, or its Source.

Conclusion

So the quest to be connected to the Source is always a struggle. A paradigm for that struggle is in the Old Testament story of Jacob and his wrestling match with the mysterious messenger of God.

It was a long, hard night for Jacob, and at times it looked like he would win the match. When daylight came, the angel disabled Jacob with just a touch, but Jacob still would not let go, saying, "I will not let you go, unless you bless me" (Gen. 32:26).

Jacob never did learn the name of the one with whom he wrestled that night, but he went away from that confrontation having been given a new name, for the mystical stranger had changed his name from Jacob to Israel. Israel means "he who contends with God" or, if you please, "he who wrestles or struggles with God." All seekers after the Source are destined to be wrestlers with God. It's always love/hate, beauty/terror, faith/doubt. And we, like Jacob, can only hope to go limping into the Promised Land, wounded but blessed.

So, if your god is too small, why don't you pick on somebody your own size—or bigger? Why don't you choose a God worthy of your love and your contending? Your image of God is really subjective—remember that God cannot be defined or understood—therefore, what you think about God is really what you think about yourself. The spirit that is you is the closest thing you have that is made of the same substance as God, you are indeed a chip off the old block. If your vision of God is narrow, revengeful, petty, unforgiving, and trite, you have in fact said more about your pitiful little spirit than anything else. If your vision of God is rather nebulous, undefined, and fuzzy, it's probably a reflection of the condition of your spiritual consciousness—but there is hope. If your God is the grand and glorious Author of all Creation, the One whose essence is love, the Unknowable One whom to know is the highest ecstasy and joy, then congratulations, you will find the struggle worth the pain. The journey will be exhilarating enough without contemplation of the destination and being connected to that Source of all being your spirit will certainly grow healthy and beautiful.

You and the Source are one. Find it. Get connected.

14

Tempo

There is an old baseball joke about a pitcher who had only one pitch, and it was a change-up. I have not only told you what the joke is about, I've told you the whole joke. If you aren't laughing, or at least indulging in a mild chuckle, it's probably because you don't understand the baseball jargon involved. A change-up pitch is a change of pace. The idea is to throw several fast balls, then one that looks like a fast ball but actually comes much slower. The batter, having established a rhythm, will swing before the ball gets there. The humor in the one-liner lies in the fact that it obviously won't work if it's the only pitch you have, it's the contrast to the other pitches that makes it tricky. It is not tricky in and of itself. Oh well, you know what they say, "If you have to explain them . . ."

I am going to suggest in this chapter that a change of pace will energize your spirit, a change either way, faster or slower. The speed is not as important as the fact of the change. Remember the change-up has no magic of its own but only in contrast to the other pitches.

I used to have a cassette player that ran just a little slow. I took it in for an adjustment, and the technician assured me that it was within allowable tolerances. But it was not within my allowable tolerance. It ran too slow. It spoiled the enjoyment I found in my tapes. So I threw it away. Its degree of variance was too small for the diagnostic machine to see. But in my ears, it made all the difference.

Did you ever go to a church where they sing the Doxology too slowly? Somehow it's hard to sing, "Praise God from whom all blessings flow," with joy and feeling at the speed of a funeral dirge. I have been in many worship services where I have wanted to scream, "Why don't you pick up the pace?" The worship would be richer and more joyous—and we would finish quicker and get to the good restaurants first.

Symphony conductor Benjamin Zander claims to have figured out the proper meaning of Beethoven's controversial tempo markings. He conducts Beethoven's Ninth Symphony in record time. A music critic was quoted as saying, "It was the most coherent performance of the Ninth I'd ever encountered. For the first time it fell into place and felt absolutely right." I suspect that if Zander's pace were the universally accepted speed, that slowing it down would produce the same positive response from the critics.

I grew up in Kansas and went to college in Southern California. One of the first things I noticed while walking across campus between classes was that everyone walked faster than I did. Little short girls would brush me off the sidewalk as they hurried by. It had nothing to do with getting to class on time, I always got to class on time, even at my casual pace. It occurred to me that there was a rhythm about life that we each adopt and assume as normal, not just normal, but proper.

I have noticed that the speed I drive on the freeway is always the correct speed. I look with equal disdain on those turtles who are driving slower than me and those speed demons who are driving faster. My pace is proper no matter what it is. I have two cars, one a station wagon and one a sports car. When I am driving the sports car, the pace I set as proper is faster than when I am in the station wagon, so I encounter more people driving too slowly when I am in that car.

Once when driving the Fiat on an open stretch of interstate, cruising comfortably at about seventy miles an hour, a Porsche passed me, followed closely by a 300ZX and a Corvette. I decided to join the trio rather than look with disdain on them for speeding.

Even though my little Fiat was a bit outclassed, I stuck my foot in it and discovered that it would hum along in the ninety-mile-per-hour range right along with the big boys. What's more, it felt good, the speed limit notwithstanding.

I don't drive ninety miles an hour very much, it's not my comfortable pace, but as a change of pace it was exhilarating. I was surprised to discover that those people driving those overpriced, overpowered cars quickly began to seem like comrades, indeed old friends. Likewise, walking across campus, I decided to pick up the pace at least enough to keep up with the shortest-legged women on the path. It was energizing! I still prefer a slow stroll, it's my natural pace, but to pick up the pace once in a while is a surprisingly invigorating experience.

There is a metaphor here. All of us have a pace at which we function best, sort of a rhythm to our lives. Imagine a continuum. At the extreme ends of this continuum are people I call "pitiful" and "superterrific." You know these people. The pitiful ones are always moaning and complaining about the difficulty of life and move through it at the speed of a slug, never having a chance to grasp any of the opportunities that come by. The superterrific ones are those who are always bursting with enthusiasm, energy, and soon-to-be-realized opportunity. All pain is growing pain, all failure is learning experience, all disappointment is redirected opportunity.

To my way of thinking, both of these extremes are equally obnoxious. You don't dare ask either of them, "How are you?" for fear they will tell you. Happily, most people are somewhere toward the middle of the continuum, and we move around on it depending on what time of day it is or how much we have to accomplish or how we feel about how much we have accomplished. My suggestion is that you identify where you are on the continuum and move one notch up. Pick up the pace one beat. Anymore than that would be phony. If you speed up a tape too much, it sounds like Alvin and the Chipmunks.

I find it necessary to do that particularly in the morning. You see, I'm not a morning person. I drift through a purple haze of semi-consciousness for several hours before emerging into the blinding light of reality around the crack of noon. I am in full agreement with W. H. Auden who observed, "The reason the rooster greets the morning so enthusiastically is because he has a brain the size of a pea." But my job requires that I function, interact, relate, and, yes, even communicate during those awful prenoon hours. So I intentionally pick up the pace. I walk a bit faster than my typical morning rhythm. I pretend to be a bit cheerier than I really feel. I shake hands more vigorously and smile more quickly. The response I get from other people far outdistances the amount of extra energy invested. I picked up the Doxology just one beat, and the world comes back to me with the Hallelujah Chorus! It's like an investment. Zero multiplied by a million is still zero. One multiplied by a million . . . well, you get the picture.

People are drawn to energy like bugs to a porch light. If you pick up the pace just one beat, it makes you look like a fireball to your peers who lag slightly behind. The world is like a kid on a bicycle trying to grab onto a slow-moving truck. He can't risk a truck that is moving too fast, but one moving too slowly is of no use at all. Try this technique and take careful mental note of the responses of the people around you. A quicker step, a lighter speech cadence, and cheerier disposition, they all send signals that are read by the subconscious minds of others, and people will respond to you accordingly. In the same way, you have fooled other people, you can also fool your own spirit. Simply because you are acting more upbeat you will begin to feel more upbeat. In *Feeling Good*, Dr. David Burns has written, "The relationship between your thoughts, feelings, and behaviors is reciprocal— all your emotions and actions are the results of your thoughts and attitudes. Similarly, your feelings and behavior patterns influence your perceptions in a wide variety of ways. It follows that all emotional change is ultimately brought about by cognitions; changing your behavior will help you feel better about yourself."

So visualize a circle of interrelating influences. In the circle are feelings, thoughts, and actions. You can break into the circle anywhere you want; change one and it will change them all. If you change your actions (pick up the pace), your feelings and thoughts will follow and your spirit will be energized.

Just as beneficial as picking up the pace is slowing it down. My wife has found a certain tranquility by driving fifty-five miles per hour on the freeway, that is, the speed limit. Of course, almost everyone else considers her a slow-moving fool as they go zipping by, but she arrives at her work within minutes of them and entirely unruffled. She has released herself from the stress of jockeying in and out of the fast lanes and the worry about the highway patrolman who creeps up in your rearview mirror. She just puts it over in the slow lane and goes the speed limit; that has improved her whole day.

There are times when just slowing down puts things back in perspective and enables you to be present to the world and to the moment. The neighborhood in which I live is home to lots of very expensive cars, the Mercedes and the BMW's are more ubiquitous here than the Fords and Chevys in most communities. The aggregate value of my two cars would not buy the hubcaps for most of them. Yet I get around town with almost the same ease and comfort as they do. So I asked myself the question, "Why would one pay $50,000 for a car, when my $1,000 car does the same job?" The only possible answer must be that driving an expensive car somehow enhances the driving experience, it lends more joy to the process of getting from point "A" to point "B." Yet to look at the faces of those drivers as they burn up the side streets and coast through the stop signs, one could not recognize any signs of joy in the process. They are so anxious to get to where they are going, they don't even notice the process. I suspect that the reason people pay extra for turbo-charged engines is so they can get it up to seventy miles per hour between the stop signs. It's necessary to have more and more powerful cars as the stop signals get closer together.

Perhaps if they would slow down, be present to the moment, enjoy the smooth hum of the engine, the responsive handling, the feel and smell of authentic Italian leather seats, the flowing grain of the mahogany dashboard, the rich full sound of the six-channel stereo, then the investment would be worthwhile. The healthy spirit must slow down from time to time and focus not so much on where it is going but where it is.

Sometimes God intervenes and blesses us by shaking up our usual, hectic pace and forcing us to function differently, whether we like it or not. Of course we never see it as a blessing at the time.

We fume and grumble and give ourselves a head start on ulcers over those little disruptions. It's only sometime later that we discover the blessing in those times. And, of course, we never learn from the experience. The next interruption that comes along, we fume and grumble all over again.

For example, as I have said, I have two cars. I hope you don't think I have overworked the automobile analogy in this chapter, but it seems to keep working for me. When you have two cars it's dangerous to park them close to one another because they will plot against you overnight. That may sound like an extreme case of automotive paranoia, but how else could anyone explain the fact that both of my cars broke down at the same time, suffering from the same ailment? There was the Ford sitting in front of the garage, its cooling system slowly draining down the driveway, and the Fiat sitting by the curb, its cooling system draining down the gutter. The two green streams mingled in front of my house and hurried on down to the storm drain at the end of the block, effectively rendering me transportationless.

Those of you who are carwise are saying to yourselves, "It's his own dumb fault for his choice of cars." Yes, I know that "Ford" is an acronym of "Fix or Repair Daily" and "Fiat" is an acronym of "Fix It Again, Tony." I admit my complicity in my dilemma. It's even worse than you think; I traded an MG for the Fiat! It's a little like trading a Studebaker for an Edsel, but that's another story for another time.

The point is that I was on foot. It takes a moment for the reality of that statement to sink in in Southern California. It was a mile and a half to work. I could walk, but what if someone I knew saw me! It could destroy my professional credibility. Don't misunderstand me, walking is an honorable activity in my neighborhood, but you must be wearing a hundred-dollar jogging outfit while you are doing it. That's a signal that you are health conscious and in step with the spirit and style of Southern California suburbia. But if you are walking, wearing a suit and tie, that's another story. The signal you send is entirely different and entirely negative. It means that you either don't have a car or have failed to maintain properly the most valuable piece of business equipment in the State of California. To be wheel-less is to be suspect. It calls into question one's ability to function as a part of civilized society. A peripatetic preacher is anachronistic indeed.

But I set out on the walk keeping to the back streets as best I could. Within yards of my house I began to see things I had never seen before, the colors and shapes of things, the plants and the trees. I noticed the way the streets curved, the brickwork in some of the driveways. I saw some whole houses I had never noticed before. It was like *Brigadoon* in my own community. I was surprised at how wide the street was when you walk across it, and I observed for the first time how the crosswalk lines were painted.

A squirrel winked at me from his burrow near the tennis court. I was discovering things he had known all along, and I guess he wanted to gloat a little. A van came down the street creating such a draft that my hair stood up for a moment and my tie blew over my shoulder. I wonder if the van driver was aware of the experience he had created for me? I wonder if he saw my tie follow him? I wonder if he saw me at all? I know he didn't see the squirrel, and the squirrel didn't wink at him. But I winked at the squirrel as he, surprised by the sudden intrusion of the van, scurried for the safety of his hole in the ground. And I smiled, for his hair and mine had stood up for exactly the same instant. We were as one, caught up in the same wind, the same spirit, the same moment in time. Because my pace had been forcibly slowed by the tyranny of the inanimate object, I was more at one with that little hairy creature than with the other member of my species driving the speed machine. It was a moment! A moment not to be shared by any other person because they were all moving too fast; they existed in another dimension of time.

I remember an old "Star Trek" episode in which the crew of the *Enterprise* comes upon a whole society of people who appeared to be frozen like statues. Looking away and looking back again they observed that the statues had changed positions. They were moving, but ever so slowly. They existed in another dimension of time. The script left unanswered the question of whether the slow movers could also see the *Enterprise* crew members or if they appeared to them as if someone had pressed the fast-forward button.

The miracle that had enabled me to see with new eyes, to commune with a different part of creation, to discover a world within a world I had never noticed before was just slowing down. It was like time travel, and the vehicle was the change of pace.

I was flying at 36,000 feet over Arizona when the pilot announced that the passengers seated on the left side of the aircraft had an excellent view of Phoenix and the passengers on the right side could see Tucson. People looked up from their *Wall Street Journals*, some for a full fifteen seconds or so, so that they could fully experience Tucson, Arizona. But I've been on the ground in Tucson, on foot in Tucson, I've seen it up close and personal, as a sports announcer used to say. I know that you could spend a lifetime and not fully experience Tucson. Yet we were told, and some of us believed, that we had an "excellent view" for fifteen seconds from 36,000 feet.

I was tempted to ask the person in the window seat if he had met my brother while he was experiencing Tucson. My brother is an interesting man, works as a meat cutter in a supermarket, goes bowling on Friday nights, sings in his church, and has raised six kids. In order to really experience Tucson, you would need to get to know my brother, or someone like him. But I don't suppose he managed that in those fifteen seconds. Of course, the people on the left side of the plane didn't experience Tucson at all, they got Phoenix instead.

On the return trip we were told with delight that we had a crystal clear view of the Grand Canyon. Everybody rushed to a window at that announcement, Everybody, that is, except me. You see, I had seen the Grand Canyon up close and personal. I had experienced it in the dimension of time in which it truly exists. I started down on foot in the early morning hours, every curve in the path revealing new vistas and shapes and colors, wildlife and plants.

Just when you think you are near the bottom, a whole new gorge opens up beneath you, and the adventure is on again. At the bottom I shared lunch with fellow time travelers from all over the world. Then, loaded with water, I started to climb out knowing that even though it was just past noon, I would be in a race with the sun. The path I chose for the climb out was steeper and hotter than could be imagined. There were times when I fell exhausted in any scrap of shade I could find and, with my sides heaving, declared that the canyon had won. I was defeated. But the canyon and I were not adversaries, we existed in the same dimension of time, and she beckoned me onward and upward, and I reached the top just as some tourists were gathering to watch the sunset on Inspiration Point. I smirked at their silliness. They thought they could sit on a rock within a hundred yards of their air-conditioned cars and experience the Grand Canyon. The canyon and I knew better, so I brushed by them without so much as a nod, and a squirrel winked at me.

A change of pace will change your perceptions, change your life, set your spirit free. In music, pace is called tempo. It's one of the major components of music along with pitch and rhythm. If life is analogous to a symphony, then, the tempo of life must be a primary consideration. And everyone who has ever been to a symphony knows that nothing is quite so exciting in a musical score as a change of tempo.

> Be aware of the pace at which you travel through life and, from time to time, change it.

15

Lean on Me

*T*hen the LORD God said, 'It is not good that the man should be alone; I will make him a helper fit for him'" (Gen. 2:18). We are created a relational being. Since that moment at the dawn of time when God breathed the breath of life into that pile of dirt and we became living souls, we have needed a helper, a comforter, someone to share with, to challenge us, to help define us, someone to lean on. At the exact same time that God created humankind, He also invented the family and the community. We are designed and built for relationship. Outside of relationships it is impossible to be at our best. We are like parts of a machine; we function as part of the whole. Separate from that mechanism we have no purpose. As Paul said, we are like a body, but we can't all be eyes and feet in order to function. If the eyes and feet are disconnected from the body, they are useless. If you are feeling poorly physically, emotionally, and spiritually, it could be that you have become disconnected from your community. The healthy spirit knows that, more than most anything else, we need each other.

We need to be touched and affirmed. We need to be needed by each other. Most of the good stuff that is in each of us presents itself only in community. Have you noticed how just saying how you feel to another person brings healing? It doesn't even have to be someone you know—a priest behind a screen, a chaplain assigned to you. Scott Peck, in his book about community, *The Different Drum*, has made it clear that creating real community can be difficult, even threatening. It involves the risk of self-disclosure and the resultant vulnerability. He writes: "Remember that community is a state of being together in which people, instead of hiding behind their defenses, learn to lower them, in which instead of attempting to obliterate their differences, people learn not only to accept them but rejoice in them." Some people, finding real friendships too threatening, choose to have acquaintances instead, sometimes lots of them, but no one to lean on when the chips are down, no one who knows their heart.

Particularly during times of personal trauma or sadness the work of relationship seems too much to tackle. As a result, at times when we most need community (and the healing it brings), it is not there.

We isolate ourselves precisely at the moments when we most need the healing of interaction and the cleansing of vulnerability. When we are sad, depressed, or disappointed, we tend to add loneliness to our troubles. We justify it to ourselves saying that we wouldn't be very good company or we don't want to bore other people with our problems. But that's not really it. Our problem is really the fear of being vulnerable, of giving up that image we project among our friends of our being strong, capable, in control, and jolly. I have been deeply cleansed by a good cry in solitude and aloneness, but it doesn't quite compare to the joy of a tear shared with a caring friend.

Of course, interaction is not just for hard times. Good times shared are a joy multiplied. There is an old joke about a preacher who skipped church on a Sunday morning so he could go golfing. God and Saint Peter saw him and agreed that he should be punished. The preacher teed up at the first fairway. The ball flew straight as an arrow for 425 yards and rolled into the cup. Saint Peter said, "A hole in one is hardly punishment." God replied, "Oh, yes it is. Who's he going to tell?" When good things happen to you, you need to tell someone. Everything is more fun if it's shared. Grief shared is divided; joy shared is multiplied.

In *Will You Be My Friend?* James Kavanaugh wrote: "Friendship is freedom, is flowing, is rare. It does not need stimulation, it stimulates itself. It trusts, understands, grows, explores, it smiles and weeps. It does not exhaust or cling, expect or demand. It is—and that is enough—and it dreams a lot."

A friend is someone who knows all your faults and likes you anyhow. A friend is someone who knows the song of your heart and will sing it to you when you forget the tune. Perhaps the best things said about friendship, community, and relationship have been said by poets. Songwriter Paul Williams penned these words in "That's What Friends Are For":

> Friends are like music,
> Sometimes they're sad,
> Sometimes they're lonely
> And need to be told that they're loved.
> Everyone needs to be loved.
> Friends are like good wine,
> And I've had the best.
> Don't always show it,
> But no one knows better than I.
> Friends are like warm clothes in the night air,
> Best when they're old
> And you miss them the most when they're gone.
> Friends love your good side
> And live with your bad,
> Want you and need you
> When no one else knows you're alive.

What we've said so far in this chapter isn't controversial. Everyone agrees that relationships are everything, that love is the stuff of life, that hard times are easier when you have someone to lean on, that good times are better shared with friends, that the work of relationship is worth it, that the best songs are love songs and the best poems are about friends. Yet it seldom occurs to anyone that there may be some skills involved in acquiring and sustaining relationships, those universally acknowledged "best things in life." It seldom occurs to people that there may be ways to enhance those skills so that the end result—community—is more fulfilling and less painful to accomplish.

Most of the people that I have talked with just naturally assumed that they will be good at it. They think relationship skills are something that comes with the human package, something that we inherit as a birthright. All one needs to do is look around. It should be brutally apparent that such is not the case. If it were, there would not be so much loneliness, alienation, and divorce in the world nor would there be so many sickly spirits. Still we go on in our personal lives as if good relationships will happen naturally and all the right skills and instincts will be there at our command when we need them. Think again!

In anything we do, we expect to get some training for it along the way. When you wanted to drive a car, you took a class, you didn't just assume that your foot would instinctively know the gas pedal from the brake and that all the right responses would be there. Skill in driving is a matter of training and practice, as is operating a computer or playing a musical instrument. The analogies are endless. Yet when it comes to that skill that we all agree is most intimately related to our happiness, our mental and spiritual well-being, our sense of personal worth, namely, the establishing and sustaining of good, healthy relationships, we rely on luck or chance or a rabbit's foot to get us by. I think a course on interpersonal relationships ought to be required in every elementary school. More advanced courses should be taught all through the school curriculum. Relationships should become the fourth "R."

"Relationships" should be seen as a skill every bit as basic and essential to us as math and reading because it is absolutely necessary if one is to succeed in life both on a personal and a professional level. If the task of education is to prepare students to live successfully in our society, why should it ignore the most basic skill that makes for a community and a society? Mostly it's left to chance; some get lucky and get good at it, perhaps because they have good role models at home, but the rest of us spend our lives suffering from a lack of this basic, teachable skill. If you, like most of us, were never offered a course in "Relationships 101," you probably had to learn about it just like you learned about sex: in the locker room or on the streets. Most of us were self-taught if we were taught at all. Sadly, we learned through trial and error— lots of error.

Statistically, second marriages are more successful than first ones. That's not because people choose better partners the second

time but because the participants are smarter and more skilled;
they know some things about what makes a relationship work and
not work. Their expectations are more realistic. They have learned
techniques, and they know when and how to apply them in order
to avoid crises and make the most of good times. Interestingly,
many people choose a second mate who's just like their first. Many
have confessed to me that if they had had the skills they have now
back during their first marriage, it would have been just as easy to
make the first marriage work. There must be another way to teach
people skills besides letting them go through a disastrous marriage
and the tragedy of divorce. May I suggest at the very least we all
spend more time contemplating our relationships with our spouse,
children, parents, friends, etc. Ask yourself if they are what you
had hoped for and how they might be improved. Then ask yourself
if you possess the skill to make it happen.

The Golden Rule of Successful
Relationships Management

What I am going to offer you is so simple you may be tempted
not to take it seriously. Don't skip over this part! Read it carefully
and think about your loved ones as you read.

This Golden Rule will improve your relationships, from the
most intimate ones to the most casual. I call it the Golden Rule
because it is a variation on the one Jesus stated so simply and eloquently. For successful relationship management, do for other people what you would like to have done for yourself. We humans are a
lot alike where our needs are concerned. We all want the same
things: we want to be *noticed, valued, complimented,* and *affirmed.*

The main complaint that I hear from wives about their hus-
bands is that they don't pay attention, they don't notice things.
She spends all afternoon at the hairdresser getting a dye job with a
cut and perm. She looks great and she feels great. He comes home
and says, "Hi dear, how was your day?" and with that makes for
his chair, his paper, and his television remote control. She persists, "Don't you notice anything different?" He looks up from his
paper and in his most pleasant voice says, "New dress, very nice."
She turns away, remembering a time when their relationship was
new, when he noticed everything about her, even the subtlest

changes in her looks, her perfume, her weight. His not noticing translates to her as not caring, but he can't figure out why she seems so upset over such a little thing. If he would remember the Golden Rule, he could figure it out.

In *The Road Less Traveled*, Scott Peck says, "The principle form that the work of love takes is attention. . . . The act of attention requires that we make the effort to set aside our existing preoccupations and actively shift our consciousness. Attention is an act of will, of work against the inertia of our own minds." Another human being is a gloriously complex and mysterious place to explore, always changing and growing. Two people can go through their whole lives together and never discover all there is to know; new discoveries keep the love alive. In relationships, we find all sorts of verbal and nonverbal ways to signal one another, to entice one another, to invite one another to come and explore further. There is no greater insult than having that invitation rejected on the assumption that you've seen all there is to see. Pay attention! The mystery of growth goes on. One day you may wake up and look and find that you are married to a stranger.

After you have noticed, make sure that the other person knows you have noticed. That's called affirmation. Jesus was a master at it. As a matter of fact, if anything would describe the ministry of Jesus in one sentence, it would be that He affirmed the worth of the worthless, He hugged the untouchables. Just by His presence among them, because He paid attention to people, He enhanced their sense of self-worth, and they felt affirmed. That included the leper by the gate, the lame man by the pool, the woman at the well, and even the tax collector in the tree. Everyone was hoping Jesus wouldn't notice that little sinner up the tree, maybe the procession would just go on by. But Jesus had a way of noticing things, and He stopped to have a word with the tax collector perched in the tree. Jesus didn't scold him for his irreligious attitude or his questionable occupation. He just invited Himself over to his house for dinner. Jesus paid attention to a man who was unworthy of Him, and it turned his life around; he was affirmed.

One morning Jesus heard a commotion going on and went to see what was happening. A woman had been caught in the act of adultery and was about to be stoned for it. That was what the law prescribed. After Jesus had disarmed and dispelled the crowd with those famous words, "Let him who is without sin among you be the first to throw a stone at her" (John 8:7), He said to the woman, "Go, and do not sin again" (John 8:11). It wasn't an order or a threat; it was an affirmation. By paying attention to her, He had shown her her worth, that she was a better person than her behavior implied. "Do not sin again" was a challenge to live a life worthy of herself.

Everyone wants the same things you want: for the people they love to notice them, to respect them, and to tell them they are okay. But it's not enough just to think about it, you have to actually do it. I recommend that you do it intentionally. Make a list of the people in your life that you want to affirm and check them off one at a time. Put yourself on a schedule, one affirmation a day. Those affirmations can be as simple as a slap on the back, or a little compliment, or just taking time to stop by and say "Hello." And you don't need to worry about the process becoming artificial because you are working from a list. The feelings will follow the action.

We dealt with precisely this issue in my college psychology class. We were discussing the fact that people are affected positively when you say nice things about or to them. It seems everyone loves a compliment. So we created what we dubbed "The Campus Compliment Club." The task was to compliment someone everyday before class and then be prepared to give a report of their response. I was uneasy about the assignment. Wouldn't it be artificial and phony? That sort of thing ought to flow naturally. It seemed hypocritical to compliment someone because that was my assignment. People aren't dumb; they recognize a sincere compliment from an insincere one done to fulfill an assignment.

I learned two lessons very quickly. First, I learned that the feeling did indeed follow the action. I looked for things to compliment because it was an assignment, but the things I found were real and so were the compliments. In fact, it got to be an epidemic for me, my eyes were opened by the process. I saw behaviors, appearances, and traits worthy of compliments everywhere. It was fun for me, and people enjoyed seeing me coming.

Second, I learned that people love to be complimented, so much that they will go to great lengths to accept the compliment as true and deserved, no matter how outrageous. Try it sometime. Say to someone you know, "You're the smartest person I ever met. I wouldn't be surprised if you become president of the United States someday." They will smile and blush, and love you for it, and probably follow you home. Remember that great old Woody Allen movie, *Play It Again Sam?* Woody Allen, the anti-hero, is trying to make a move on the lovely wife of his friend. Bogart, his alter ego is giving him some pointers. She is in his apartment, the lights are low, the music is soft, his arm is around her on the couch. Bogart whispers to Woody, "Tell her you've met a lot of dames, but she's the most exciting dame you've ever met." Allen protests, "Oh, she'll never buy that." Bogey says confidently, "Try it." So Woody tries the line. She blushes and grins, and with a sigh in her voice says, "Really?" Woody Allen smiles too and says with relief, "She bought it!"

It illustrates wonderfully how hungry people are to be complimented. If people go to such lengths to accept a compliment that is obviously a line, think how they might respond to your kind and sincere observations. Pay attention, notice the good things about the people you love and let them know that you notice. If you are really bad with words let Hallmark say it for you. There are greeting cards available for most every occasion under the sun and even for no occasion at all. Those are the best!

I got a little gift from my mother once, some aftershave with a note that said, "Not for any particular occasion, just because I love you." So buy a bunch of those no-occasion cards and send them to your special friends, the ones that say "I like you," "You did a good job," "You're neat." A quarter for a stamp, a dollar for a card, and it could change your life. Get one for your wife and put it in her dresser drawer so she will find it in the morning. If you are too cheap to buy cards, use a scrap of paper, it works just as well. Go to the card shop and copy the verses. One of the best gifts I ever received was a scrap of lined paper from a little spiral notebook. It couldn't have been more welcome if it had been engraved in gold on parchment and delivered by special delivery. Instead it was paperclipped to my mail slot at the office.

The church in San Diego was a large concrete-and-glass building with all the difficult acoustical problems those buildings seem to have. We spent nearly $60,000 for a state-of-the-art sound system, which from the beginning didn't work properly. The sound consultant was fired, and I, because of my previous experience with such equipment, was made the man in charge of taming the savage beast and forcing it to serve our purposes. I spent hours of extra time alone in the sanctuary tuning and tweaking on that system. Every week we received notes in the offering plate complaining about the quality of the sound: too loud, too soft, too mushy, too shrill, too echoey. Some even threatened to start going to another church where they could at least understand what was being said. After about a year of that kind of abuse and after much overtime, I had about had it. Then came the aforementioned note, clipped to my mail slot, no envelope, just notepaper folded over. It was from one of the other ministers on the staff. It said, "Bob, some of us here are aware of, and do appreciate, the time and work you spend on the sound system." Tears welled up in my eyes. I had been noticed by a friend and colleague. I was affirmed. I drew enough strength from that note to see the process through to a time when the whole church agreed that the sound was great. It was just a little note, the cost of it could be measured in fractions of a penny, the time investment in seconds, the effect immeasurable.

There is another piece of lined, yellow notebook paper in my life. It hangs framed on my office wall. I didn't mount my diplomas or my ordination certificate, but I point to that piece of yellow paper and say, "There are my credentials." It is printed in pencil in a child's hand; the signature at the bottom belongs to Ricky. It says:

1. You are a great singer!
2. You are a great guitarist!
3. You are a great player!
4. You are a great minister!
5. You are great!
6. You do good prayers!!
7. You are a super guy!!!!!!!!
8. You do good riddles!!
9. You are super!!!!!!!!!!!!!!
10. You are very very great!!!!!!!!!!

At the bottom there is a drawing of a flower garden, and the biggest flower in the garden has my name on it and a butterfly.

I don't remember who Ricky was, but he surely did affirm my worth. The yellow paper came in the offering plate at a church in Michigan where I was singing and speaking. As is my practice, I took it home and put it on my refrigerator door. It disappeared after a couple of months, swept into the wastebasket, I assumed. It was later presented to me, professionally framed, by the woman who became my wife. I was twice affirmed with that yellow piece of paper—both by Ricky and by Louise—and I smile and think of them warmly every time I glance up from my desk and see the biggest flower drawn in pencil, the one with the butterfly.

I warned you earlier that these kinds of considerations were so simple that you might not take them seriously. Although they are simple and inexpensive, they require the work of attention. But it is time and work all rewarded in richer and sweeter relationships.

One of my favorite Old Testament stories is the story of Naaman (2 Kings 5). Naaman was a general in the Syrian army, a man of great power and respect, but he was a leper. On one of their raids into Israel, they carried off a little girl who became Naaman's servant. She commented one day that there was a prophet in Israel who could heal Naaman of his leprosy. So Naaman gathered up all his army and regalia, loaded down the caravan with expensive gifts and headed for Israel to ask the king for healing. The king thought he was either kidding or looking for an excuse to attack. Then the word came that Naaman should take his request to the prophet Elisha. So Naaman, with his whole entourage of chariots, warriors, horses, and treasures, went rumbling off into the woods to find Elisha's cabin. Elisha didn't even come out to meet the famous Syrian general, but sent out his houseboy to tell Naaman to go wash seven times in the Jordan River and he would be healed. Naaman was furious. He expected the great prophet to come out and do some fancy incantations and whip up a magic potion. He expected Elisha to ask some great feat of courage or strength of him. What about all these gifts he had brought along? Instead of that, a little boy told him to go down to the river and take a bath. He was indignant; there were better rivers in Syria for bathing. Then one of his servants spoke the words of wisdom that are the point of the whole story: "If the prophet had commanded you to do some great thing, would you not have done it? How much rather, then, when he says to you 'Wash, and be clean'?" (2 Kings 5:13).

If I were to offer you a foolproof method for improving your relationships, but you had to do some great, difficult task, or spend lots of money, or attend a weekend seminar to obtain it, you would probably do it. What I am telling you, though, is so simple, you might pass it up. What you want for yourself is what everyone else wants. So pay attention, notice people, compliment people, affirm people. Just take time to think of all the good qualities about the people who are important to you and tell them. Or just invest in a book of notepaper and a pencil. If you still can't think of anything to write, why not borrow a line from the ages: "I love you."

A preacher told me this story. It's about his first-grade schoolteacher. He said that she was one of the most important influences on his life and that she, at that early stage in his life, had done more than anyone to set him on a course that led to success and personal fulfillment. Of course he didn't realize it at the time, those realizations usually come much later. In the course of his life he figured he had made reference to her a thousand times in sermons, speeches, and casual conversations. He would often remark about her profound influence on his life until it seemed he had told everyone, everyone, that is, except her. He had read an article somewhere that said if you love someone, you are responsible for letting them know it. So he did some research and discovered that she was still living and had long since retired. He got her address and wrote her a note. In it he told her all the things he had told everyone else about how important and influential she had been in his life, about how he had referred to her a thousand times in sermons and speeches. A letter came back. In it she thanked him for his kind words. This was her closing line: "I taught school for forty years and yours is the first letter."

That's how we sin against one another; the kind word left unsaid, the affirmation unshared, the compliment unoffered. The judgment for that sin is the loss of the most joyous of all life's blessings, relationships. Relationships are the stuff of life, we need

one another, we are created that way. Take the time to take stock
of your precious relationships and begin to apply the Golden
Rule to them, and, oh yes, prayer helps too.

> If you have a friend worth loving,
> Love him. Yes, and let him know
> That you love him, ere life's evening
> Tinge his brow with sunset glow.
> Why should good words never be said
> Of a friend—till he is dead?
> If you hear a song that thrills you,
> Sung by any child of song,
> Praise it. Do not let the singer
> Wait deserved praises long.
> Why should one who thrills your heart
> Lack the joy you may impart?
> If you hear a prayer that moves you
> By its humble, pleading tone,
> Join it. Do not let the seeker
> Bow before his God alone.
> Why should not your brother share
> The strength of "two or three" in prayer?
> If you see the hot tears falling
> From a brother's weeping eyes,
> Share them. And by kindly sharing
> Own your kinship in the skies.
> Why should anyone be glad
> When another's heart is sad?
>   —Anonymous

Make a list of the people you care most about and in
the next thirty days find a way to tell them so. Make
another list of those things you wish your loved ones
would do for you and begin to do those things for
them. Then get ready for a love rush.

A "Small" Digression

Have you noticed that the word *creativity* keeps coming up in these chapters? It seems impossible to discuss the uniqueness of humankind and spiritual well-being without using that word as part of the dialogue. Nothing so defines us as spiritual beings and motivates us to pursue and enrich that spiritualness as does the ubiquitous creative instinct in us all. Our creativity is what distinguishes us from the animals and the rest of creation and aligns us with God.

Ever since I learned to fingerpaint in the first grade, I have known that creating a tree or an ocean or a world on a piece of white paper must be akin in joy to what God feels when He makes the real things. When I am creative, I feel a closeness, even a connectedness, to the source of all creativity. Creativity confirms in me the assurance that I am like Him, even part of Him. It seems, therefore, appropriate to say a few more words on the subject, even though it has been commented on in other chapters.

What Is Creativity?

The best definition I've heard of creativity is that it is the ability to look at something and see something else. Bob Kane, the creator of "Batman" some fifty years ago, got the idea when he saw a Leonardo da Vinci drawing of a man with batwings attached to his arms. Creativity stimulates creativity. Kane looked at da Vinci's sketch of a flying machine and imagined Batman. Put another way, creativity is seeing what others have seen and thinking what no one else has thought.

When you were a child, you probably used to lie on your back in the tall grass, watch the white, puffy clouds drift by and say to yourself, "There goes an elephant, or a unicorn, or a maple leaf, or a horseshoe." Anyone without a sense of creativity would hear your mutterings and think you mad, but another spirit endowed with creative vision would understand perfectly. Both would disagree with you; the first would insist that you were only looking at clouds; the second would say, "No, it's not an elephant, it's a tank, or it's not a horseshoe, it's a satin ribbon." Then there are the poor souls who don't even notice that the clouds are up there.

Michael Masser has written some of the best pop songs of the last decade. Some, like "The Greatest Love of All," were hits by several artists. I find the story behind the man to be very interesting. Masser left a successful Wall Street career to follow his creative urge. Daniel B. Wood said this about him and his creativity in the *Christian Science Monitor*: "Getting Masser to explain the technical side of constructing a song is nearly impossible. He goes to one of the two concert-size Yamaha grands in his mansion and begins pounding out chords. He speaks of stream of consciousness, instincts, dramatics, 'the music passing through me.' Soon you are aware that creativity—at least this kind of creativity—defies explanation."

Who Has Creativity?

For the answer to this question, I defer to Maxwell Maltz, who wrote in *Psycho-Cybernetics*: "We often think of 'Creative Imagination' as applying only to poets, inventors, and the like. But imagination is creative in everything we do. Although they did not understand why or how imagination sets our creative mechanism into action, serious thinkers of all ages, as well as hardheaded 'practical' men, have recognized the fact and made use of it. 'Imagination rules the world,' said Napoleon. 'Imagination of all man's faculties is the most God-like,' said Glenn Clark. 'The faculty of imagination is the great spring of human activity, and the principal source of human improvement. . . . Destroy this faculty, and the condition of man will become as stationary as that of the brutes,' said Dugold Stewart, the famous Scottish philosopher. 'You can imagine your future,' says Henry J. Kaiser, who attributes much of his success in business to the constructive, positive use of creative imagination. . . . 'Creative Imagination' is not something reserved for poets and philosophers, the inventors. It enters into our every act."

All beings who are created in the image of God have the gift of creativity. It permeates our lives and animates our day-to-day existence. We all have it; it's what defines us as who we are. The larger question is to what extent we will encourage it, celebrate it, and employ it as one of our most valuable tools in the doing of life. Or will we be tempted to bury it under layers of rational, systematic thinking, assuming it to be a useless vestige left over from childhood, something we gave up on about the same time we stopped lying on our backs in the tall grass watching cloud pictures on a summer's day?

What Makes Creativity Happen?

The answer to that question is a glorious mystery. Sigmund Freud said, "The nature of artistic attainment is psychologically inaccessible to us." That means that creativity does not fall easily under the scrutiny of the scientific method with its systems and formulas, further confirmation that creativity is a matter of the spirit.

The answer to the question is that you can't make it happen! You can't force it. You can only allow it to happen. You can make of your spirit an uncluttered, obstacle-free room, where it can enter at its own will. It happens to me when I put my mind in neutral. Some people call it the beta level of consciousness or a meditative state, some people call it daydreaming. I call it putting my mind in neutral.

It happens when I'm driving, especially those long familiar stretches. Suddenly I will realize that while part of my mind has been controlling the machine and paying attention to traffic, another part of my mind has been off doing other work, creative work. Maltz characterized the process so well in his book. It's as if we each have at our disposal an army of little creative elves who work unceasingly on the problems and tasks we assign them. They work even while we sleep. Then, once in a while, when we put our mind in neutral, the elves step forward and present us with the solution.

It is said that Thomas Edison took short naps throughout the day. His assistants first suspected him of being lazy, but he was using the creative process described by Maltz. When a problem in the laboratory had him stumped, he would assign it to his army of creative elves and let them work on it while he slept. When he woke up, the solution would be presented to him.

The elves step forward in regiments when I am driving. I often carry a notebook or a tape recorder because I know that once they present the answer to a particular assignment, they are not likely to do it again. I look forward to those long drives because of the anticipation of being in dialogue with my creative self.

It happens at other times too. One whole chapter of this book came to me while I was walking. All I did was go to the office and write it down. I'm going to give part of the royalty to the elves' union.

It also happens, I'm embarrassed to say, when I am listening to other people speak. The chair is comfortable, the room warm, the speaker's voice a hypnotic drone, and the first thing I know I'm off to creative dialogue land. I hope any of my church members who read this will have the courtesy not to tell me whether they do that when I am preaching. Realistically, it can happen whether the speaker is boring or interesting. That's because the mind can think faster than the mouth can speak. So the mind figures out in advance how the sentence is going to end and then goes looking for something else to do in the meantime. Finding that activity of infinitely more interest, it refuses to come back for the beginning of the next sentence. There are techniques that speakers use to bring listeners back when we see them off in their independent imaginary world. For me the most effective method of retrieving the strays is a long silence. The mind comes rushing back to see what happened—did the record stop, did the microphone break, did the preacher lose his place, and, God forbid, did he ask me a question? Sometimes I just leave them out there on their separate journeys. There are times when people depart to be in communication with their creative elves and end up in communion with the Holy Spirit, who might say things to them of infinitely more importance than the substance of my little sermon. Those same creative channels are the lines that God uses to speak to our hearts and soothe our spirits. Our creativity is that which most closely relates us to God.

Sometimes it happens when I am in the shower. I'm not yet quite awake. The warm water rushing over me—it's as close as a grown person can get to reexperiencing the womb. Yesterday I had read the Scripture lesson for next Sunday's sermon, and this morning before breakfast my elves came into my bathroom to hand me a finished manuscript. All I had to do was get dressed and write it down.

Wolfgang Mozart said, "When I am . . . completely myself, entirely alone . . . or during the night when I cannot sleep, it is on such occasions that my ideas flow best and most abundantly. Whence and how these come I know not nor can I force them." Anton Bruckner was asked where he got the inspiration for his Ninth Symphony. "Well, it was like this," Bruckner replied. "I walked up the Kahlenberg, and when it got hot and I got hungry, I sat down by a little brook and unpacked my Swiss cheese. And just as I open the greasy paper, that darn tune pops into my head!"

You can't make creativity happen; you can only let it happen. I believe that it happens best for people who cultivate an active curiosity. Creativity and curiosity fuel each other. That's why it is so important not to stifle the curiosity of children even if it expresses itself as mischief. I agree with whoever said, "There is a correlation between the creative and the screwball, so we must suffer the screwball gladly."

In *A Whack on the Side of the Head*, Roger Van Oech recalls Carl Ally, a successful advertising agency founder, saying, "The creative person wants to be a know-it-all. He wants to know about all kinds of things: ancient history, nineteenth-century mathematics, current manufacturing techniques, flower arranging, and hog futures. Because he never knows when these ideas might come together to form a new idea."

Creativity is an ongoing process that requires constant fuel. In the movie *Short Circuit*, a robot comes to life and immediately is starved for input. In fact, it is that craving for input that is the principal evidence for its being alive. The highest expression of life is creativity, and its fuel is input, stimulus, and experiences gathered in by an active, searching curiosity.

Can Creativity Be Lost?

Creativity cannot be forced, but it can be stifled. What an ironic tragedy that this stifling often happens in schools. Programs in the creative arts are always the first to go when funding is cut. These kinds of courses are never required, but the rational disciplines are held as indispensable. Teachers, themselves thus schooled, become totally oriented around right-answers kinds of thinking, and rewards are handed out accordingly. Just once I'd like to see an award given for the most creative answer to a math question. The creative thinker is pushed to the side of the fast track to success. His inborn creative urge being unrewarded is buried and then dies.

Once I substitute taught in an elementary art class. I asked the students to show me the pictures they had done the day before. One was reluctant to show me his picture and after some coaxing I discovered that it was because his regular teacher had criticized his picture for its inaccuracy. I finally convinced him to show it to me. It looked like a seven-legged, purple cow. I said, "It looks like a seven-legged, purple cow!" He said, "That's what it is." "Why didn't your teacher like it?" I inquired. He said, "She said there was no such thing as a seven-legged, purple cow." "What did you say?" I said. He answered, "Sure there is, see here!"

Harry Chapin wrote a poignant little song about that same issue. The chorus goes:

> Red flowers are red, young man,
> and green leaves are green.
> And there's no need to see flowers
> any other way than the way
> they always have been seen.

S. I. Hayakawa said, "If you see in any given situation only what everybody else can see, you can be said to be so much of a representative of your culture that you are a victim of it." Rudolf Flesch said, "Creative thinking may mean simply the realization that there's no particular virtue in doing things the way they always have been done."

Fortunately the little boy in Harry Chapin's song had a resilient spirit, and he responded to the teacher:

> There are so many colors in the rainbow,
> so many colors in the morning sun,
> so many colors in the flowers
> and I see every one.

Roger Van Oech shared this sad story in his book *A Whack on the Side of the Head*: "When I was a sophomore in high school, my English teacher put a small chalk dot on the blackboard. He asked the class what it was. A few seconds passed and then someone said, 'A chalk dot on the blackboard.' The rest of the class seemed relieved that the obvious had been stated, and no one else had anything more to say. 'I'm surprised at you,' the teacher told the class. 'I did the same exercise yesterday with a group of kindergartners and they thought of fifty different things the chalk mark could be: An owl's eye, a cigar butt, the top of a telephone pole, a star, a pebble, a squashed bug, a rotten egg, and so on. They really had their imaginations in high gear.' In the ten-year period between kindergarten and high school, not only had we learned how to find the right answer, we had also lost the ability to look for more than one right answer. We had learned how to be specific, but we had lost much of our imaginative power. As noted educator Neil Postman has remarked, 'Children enter school as question marks and leave as periods.'"

Paul Simon said in a rather harsh song lyric, "When I think back on all the crap I learned in high school, it's a wonder I can think at all." Of course, schools are not the only villain; indeed in some cases they are shining examples where creativity flourishes. Let it be said that creativity must be valued and encouraged in all parts of society, not just in schools but in social, political, economic, and religious life. Let it also be said that there is a resilience about the creative spirit that can rise above negative influences. Anna Freud said, "Creative minds always have been known to survive any kind of bad training." Let us pray that she is correct.

Finally

The creative spirit looks at something and sees something else. To paraphrase Robert Kennedy's paraphrase of George Bernard Shaw, the creative spirit, rather than looking at what is and asking why, dreams of what never was and asks why not? The creative spirit surveys the world around us from the magnificent vantage point God has given us and asks the question "What if?" What if we built wings for ourselves? Could we fly? What if we created a system of government where everyone had a voice and the government existed by the consent of the governed? Would there be anarchy? What if we split the atom? Would that start an irreversible chain reaction? What if we put a man on the moon? Would he step in green cheese? What if we tried to feed the world and eliminate starvation from the planet? What if we began to treat our traditional enemies as friends? What if we saw other people as having the same needs and wants as ourselves?

Richard Bach's little book *Illusions* is subtitled *The Adventures of a Reluctant Messiah*. It asks the question, What if the messiah decided he didn't want the job? What if while he was teaching on the hillside, he just said, "I quit," and walked away? What if there was a messiah's handbook which explained how the job was to be performed and brought to light the great truths of the universe? That's the premise of Bach's creative little book. The end of the book, however, takes a creative turn. The last entry in the messiah's handbook reads, "Everything in this book may be wrong." Those who would dare ask the question "what if?" also risk asking the painful question "what if I'm wrong?"

Creativity is and always has been our greatest hope if we are to continue and prosper as a society. The ability to ask "what if" is the key to evaluating past procedures and presuppositions and imagining new and more relevant ones. What if the way we have always done things no longer works? What if all the values and principles we hold as universally true are now, because the world has turned, false? What if we look at ourselves as we are and imagine a whole new way of being?

In *The Courage of Conviction*, Jane Goodall has written eloquently of that great hope:

> Less than a hundred years ago, in our Western culture, children were sent down the mines and up the chimneys, and shivered with blue feet and rags in the snow. There were unspeakable slums, and slavery was accepted. The modern welfare state, for all its drawbacks, is certainly a step in the right direction. Our predecessors emerged triumphantly from the teeth of mighty Tyrannosaurus rex. God willing, we will also emerge from the dark menace of nuclear war. We do not (so far as we know) have any choice as to the circumstances of our birth and this has an overriding influence on the pattern of our lives. The son of a Russian peasant has very different opportunities from those of an American millionaire's child. But no matter in what position we find ourselves, we can exercise our human birthright—free will. Life offers a continual succession of choice points: Do this? or that? Speak? or keep silent? To be? or not to be?—And so, while I believe that God wills the ultimate destiny of the human race, I feel sure that the destiny of each of us as an individual lies in our own hands: to succeed or fail, love or hate, create or destroy.

Creativity, the thing about us that is most divine, is also the force that will empower us to move on; it will rescue us from our present desperate situation in the world and enable us to achieve higher heights, and remake our world into a safer, more lovely, more caring place. What if we tried to make the world look more like the Kingdom of God? Creativity, our greatest joy, our most divine attribute, may also be our salvation.

> Do something creative every day: painting, dance, music, poetry, flower arranging, rearranging the furniture. The opportunities are everywhere at home, at work, in between. Creativity is your most divine attribute. Celebrate it, and it will beautify your spirit.

─── 16 ───

A Prescription:
Sing, Dance, and Laugh

At this point in the discussion, let me offer you my prescription for a more joyous life and a lighter spirit: sing, dance, and laugh.

Laugh

William James said, "I don't laugh because I feel good, I feel good because I laugh." Earlier I talked at some length about the value of developing a sense of humor about oneself and seeing life as play. These are not the same things. You can see the humor in things without actually laughing, and you can laugh without seeing the humor in things. In that chapter, seeing the humor was the goal, in this chapter the laugh itself is the goal whether anything is funny or not. It is said that "He who laughs last probably didn't understand the joke." I am suggesting quite literally that you laugh even if nothing is funny, or perhaps especially if nothing is funny.

It turns out that the old saying is right: laughter is the best medicine. Norman Cousins has documented that truth in his little book *Anatomy of an Illness*, and if you haven't read it yet, I recommend it to you. In it Cousins described how he literally laughed himself healthy and documented the amazing medicinal effects of laughter: "I made the joyous discovery that ten minutes of genuine belly laughter had an anesthetic effect and would give me at least two hours of pain-free sleep." In developing his thesis, Cousins quotes from much older sources to make similar points:

> Immanuel Kant, in his *Critique of Pure Reason*, wrote that laughter produces a "feeling of health through the furtherance of the vital bodily processes, the affection that moves the intestines and the diaphragms; in a word, the feeling of health that makes up the gratification felt by us; so that we can thus reach the body through the soul and use the latter as the physician of the former."

More recently science has discovered the endorphin system and knows that laughter releases this healing power into the bloodstream. But the point is that it doesn't matter why it works, as long as it works. Also, your system doesn't care if the laughter is authentic or trumped up, the effect is the same. So go ahead, fool your little endorphins, laugh even when nothing is funny and let the healing power flow.

I recommend that you don't do this a lot in public places like concert halls, buses, or elevators; impromptu laughter makes the world nervous. As G. K. Chesterton has pointed out, you can get away with a smile in public, but an out-and-out laugh is suspect. In *The Common Man*, he said:

> The tendency of recent culture has been to tolerate the smile but discourage the laugh. There are three differences involved here. First, that the smile can unobtrusively turn into the sneer; second, that the smile is always individual and even secretive, while the laugh can be social and gregarious, and is perhaps the one genuine surviving form of the General Will; and third, that laughing lays itself open to criticism, is innocent and unguarded, has the sort of humanity which has always something of humility. . . . Therefore, in this modern conflict between the Smile and the Laugh, I am all in favor of Laughing. Laughter has something in it in common with the ancient winds of faith and inspiration; it unfreezes pride and unwinds secrecy; it makes men forget themselves in the presence of something greater than themselves.

So a laugh in public may make a public statement or cause a public scene, but a laugh in private works just as well in the enriching of the spirit. Perhaps, you could schedule a laugh while you are driving to work or better yet first thing in the morning; have your first cup of coffee and your first laugh to get your day started off right. You can increase the effect by looking in the mirror while you do it. If your face looks anything like mine first thing in the morning, you have to laugh to keep from crying. Laugh at least once a day. If the day goes by and you haven't laughed yet, have a big laugh before you drift off to sleep. And so my prescription for a healthy spirit includes at least one good laugh a day. If something is funny and you laugh, that is fine. If nothing is funny, laugh anyway. It's good for you.

Many others agree and have said:

Laughter is a tranquilizer with no side effects.
                                                    —*Arnold Glason*

Laughter is the sensation of feeling good all over and showing it principally in one place.
                                                    —*Josh Billings*

A good laugh is sunshine in a house.
                                    —*William Makepeace Thackeray*

Two things reduce prejudice—education and laughter.
                                                    —*Laurence J. Peter*

A laugh is like a love affair in that it carries a man completely off his feet; a laugh is like a creed or a church in that it asks that a man should trust himself to it.
                                                    —*G. K. Chesterton*

Sing

Sing once a day. I don't care how your voice sounds or whether you can carry a tune in a bucket, just open up and let it fly. That's why God created big stereo speakers and 200 watt amps: to drown out people like you. A folk singer on "Prairie Home Companion" said that he believed that everyone should sing all of the time. "If God gave you a lovely singing voice, it's a great way to say thank you and if He didn't it's a great way to get even." Dan Burton, the organist at my church in San Diego, said, "Music is God's original means of communication. It was only after man fell from his original perfection that it became necessary to develop language."

Sing in the shower—everyone sounds good in that echoey setting. Sing in the car with the windows up. If this is too radical a step for you who haven't taken aim at a musical note in years, you may want to break in by humming. Humming is singing with your mouth shut. It represents a smaller commitment on your part since most of the time other people won't be able to tell where it's coming from. Whistling also counts, but keep in mind that whistling makes your mouth look funny. I was in a supermarket checkout line, sort of humming to myself; it was a tune known only to my innermost being. The checker commented that I must really be having a good day. I told her that in fact I was having a lousy day and that's why I was doing therapy. I don't hum because I feel good; I feel good because I hum. (Pardon the paraphrase.)

Just as I provided a gallery of authoritative sources to support my thesis on laughing, I would like to introduce two persons in support of therapeutic singing who have equally impressive credentials. They are Orel Hershiser and the angel Gabriel.

Orel Hershiser is a pitcher for the L.A. Dodgers, and he won most of professional baseball's awards in 1988. There was a moment in the '88 World Series when it looked like none of that would happen for Orel. It was in the fifth game of the Series when Hershiser started to walk people. It looked like he was losing his control. The relief pitchers began warming up in the bull pen. Tommy LaSorda, the Dodgers' manager, was up pacing and looking very nervous. More than 50,000 Oakland fans were chanting his name in a singsong fashion to try to break his concentration. Everything depended on his throwing the ball hard and with perfect accuracy. If he succeeded, he would win the World Series. What was going on with Orel Hershiser at that moment is known to all of us as stress. We all know that nothing produces so many negative endorphins in our system as stress.

In one dramatic moment, Orel stepped off the mound, closed his eyes for a moment, and took some deep breaths. Then he went back to the mound, pitched his way out of the inning, retired the side in the ninth and won the World Series. After the game a reporter asked him what he did to release the tension in that critical eighth inning. He said, "I did what I always do. I put my head back and closed my eyes and sang a hymn." Later on "The Tonight Show," Johnny Carson asked him specifically what hymn he sang. It was the Doxology: "Praise God from whom all blessings flow." As my friend Mark Trotter put it in a sermon, "Orel hymned his way into sports history." (I am indebted to the Reverend Mark Trotter for reminding me of the Orel Hershiser story in one of his sermons.)

Of course, angels have to be great singers. Their very appearance produces stress in mortals, so they have to sing to calm us down. The shepherds were expecting another night of listening to sheep noises and keeping one eye open for wolves. What a surprise when a whole choir of angels showed up!

Talk about stress, what about poor Mary? She was just a girl, engaged to be married to a carpenter from Nazareth and had planned to settle down to a normal existence. What a shock! First the angel announces that she is pregnant (how is she going to explain that one to Joseph?), and then he announces that the child she is carrying is the Son of God. There is no way to present that kind of news other than singing it. So Gabriel sang, "Do not be afraid, for you have found favor with God," and Mary sang back antiphonally, "Behold, I am the handmaid of the Lord." Centuries later, John Lennon would borrow from the words of Mary for his classic song, "Let It Be."

So there you have it, spokespersons from two disciplines that are most highly respected in our society—sports and religion—and their unmitigated endorsement of singing as an effective stress-control technique. It doesn't have to be a hymn, but it can't hurt. That way you get a double benefit: namely, the therapy of singing and the blessing of praising God with your voice. If you can't decide what to sing, you might like to begin by borrowing a tune from Orel or Gabriel or Mary.

> Praise God from whom all blessings flow
> Praise Him all creatures here below
> Praise Him above ye heavenly hosts
> Praise Father, Son, and Holy Ghost. . . .
>
> Glory to God in the highest,
> and on earth peace among men
> with whom He is pleased. . . .
>
> My soul magnifies the Lord,
> and my spirit rejoices in God my Savior.

Dance

The third part of my prescription is dancing, and it's the hardest of the three. It can be defined as moving one's feet in a rhythmic pattern, but it has nothing whatever to do with marching, which can be defined the same way. Marching is a function of regimentation and organization; dancing is the response of a body whose spirit won't let it stand still.

I don't need to say much more about it because the benefits derived from it are like those derived from singing. It, like singing, can be done alone or in harmony, fast or slow. It, like singing, has been endorsed by a biblical great, David, the king (2 Sam. 6:14–15). The added benefit of dancing is that it is possibly better exercise than singing. It can certainly be every bit as expressive. Dancing can be defined as singing with your feet.

If you are one of those who claims to have zero rhythm or grace, there are some substitute activities: you can just jump, as in "Jumping for joy." Skipping also counts. You probably haven't skipped since you were a kid. Sometime, when no one is looking, give it a try and see if you still remember how.

Sing and dance and laugh. Do it whether you feel like it or not. If you only exercised your body when you felt like it, you would be a heap of flab. But when you force yourself to put on those jogging shoes and get out there and do those laps, you find yourself energized in a surprising way. In the same way a little song in the shower, a laugh in the car, and a little soft shoe in the hallway will energize your spirit.

> - Laugh (at least once a day)
> - Sing (at least once a day)
> - Dance (at least once a day)

The Last Chapter:
The Guarantee

At the beginning of this book I promised you a guarantee, and here it is. If you will identify just one of the things I have suggested in these chapters that you don't do much, and do it more, you will become a healthier spirit. If you will see life as a joyful game and play more, or develop a strong sense of purpose in your life, or learn to welcome loose ends, get rid of anger and jealousy, choose more worthy goals, learn to accept yourself as who you are and give life your best, get beyond your own needs and focus on the needs of others, lighten your load, develop a childlike spirit, avoid the sidetracks, get connected to the source, learn the magic of the change of pace, develop relationship skills, sing, dance, and laugh more—something good will happen to you.

If you will look at that list, find an item that just isn't like you at all, and adopt it as a project, it will enrich your spiritual well-being. Since I have defined spirit as indefinable, how will you know if you have a healthy one? Let me put it this way: You will feel better! Spirit, body, and mind are all interrelated. If one benefits, the whole being benefits. If you have a healthy spirit, it will be reflected in mind and body in ways that you can observe and others will notice, too.

How can I be so sure it will work for you? It's not as if I have introduced information that is until now unknown. You have probably heard all this before in one form or another; it's just that to do any of these things, indeed to do anything at all, requires movement, and movement is life. I believe in the healing value of change. The Apostle Paul said that to change the way you think is to change the way you are (Rom. 12:2). Movement, even lateral movement, is still life stimulating.

I've heard people describe tragedies like a house fire, the death of a parent, or a divorce as the best thing that ever happened to them. It wasn't actually the event itself that made the difference, it was that the event forced them to change, and they discovered new life. I know a divorced woman who had been married since she was sixteen. Now she is forty and single for the first time in her life. She went to school to learn to be a teacher, met new people, and heard new ideas, and a whole new life opened up for her. It wasn't the divorce; it was the change. It is, indeed, possible that had she forced herself to grow and change sooner, the divorce might have been avoided. Who would divorce such a growing, interesting, alive person as she had become?

I knew a family whose house burned. What a tragedy—all those memories and personal items gone. A year later they told me how the experience had forced them to evaluate life, what was really important. They saw that it was the family that was important. Now they spend more time together. When they go on a vacation, they don't bother to lock the door. The stuff in the house isn't that important. Their children learned the lessons too. Once the mother dropped a vase on the floor. It broke and she began to cry. Her daughter comforted her, "It's okay, Mom, it has no life."

Movement is exercise for the spirit; change, any kind of change, will set your spirit free. One of my favorite Bible stories is in the book of 1 Kings. Israel and Syria are squabbling with one another (so what's new?). The problem is that every time Syria sends over a raiding party, Elisha the prophet tells the Israelites where they are and spoils the ambush. You see, prophets are able to do that sort of thing.

So the Syrians sent a raiding party to get Elisha. Why they thought they could sneak up on Elisha is beyond me; apparently they hadn't thought it through too well. Anyhow, Elisha was ready for them and greeted them with his own little surprise: he struck them all blind. Then he led them right into downtown Samaria, the capital city of Israel. Imagine their surprise when Elisha gave them their sight back. There they were, surrounded by the entire Israelite army. The king said, "What shall we do? Lop off their heads?" and Elisha said, "No, feed them dinner and send them home." So they did.

The king of Syria was not at all pleased by this little indignity. He apparently hadn't read the part of my book about finding the humor in things. So he called up his whole army to go over to Samaria and teach those guys a lesson. They went and besieged the city. So effective was the siege, in a short time the food ran out and there were stories about people eating their children and outrageous prices being paid for a piece of pigeon poop. The king said to Elisha, "This is all your fault and tomorrow I'll have your head on a platter." Elisha countered calmly, "Tomorrow at this time you will be able to buy a loaf of bread in the city for a dime." The captain of the guard scoffed, "Not even if you open the windows of heaven is such a thing possible." Elisha pointed his bony prophetic finger and pronounced, "You will see it, but you won't eat it." A pretty tense drama!

The scene shifts just like a well-edited movie. Outside the city walls, four lepers squat in the dust. Apparently they got put out of the city because things were tough enough without these guys running around yelling, "Unclean, unclean." So there they were discussing their options, all of which seemed pretty grim. They could sneak back into the city, but everyone was starving there, so what was the point? Then one of them came up with a bright idea: "What if we go down to where the Syrians are camped? Chances are they will kill us, but that's better than starving here. And just maybe, since we look so pitiful, starving lepers that we are, maybe they will feel sorry for us and take us in." The plan was debated and this was the selling point, the final argument, the clincher: "Why do we sit here and die?" That's one of the greatest rhetorical questions in all of literature. "Why do we sit here and die?" Do something! Move! Change! Even if it's a change for the worse, even if your chance for success is one in a million, do something. It's better than sitting and dying.

You probably want to know the rest of the story. The lepers went down to the Syrian camp, and God made a miracle happen. (Miracles often happen when people move against incredible odds.)

The Syrians didn't hear the sound of the four stumbling lepers; what they heard sounded like thousands of charging foot soldiers. They ran away, leaving behind everything: gold, silver, and bread. The news was announced in the city, and the people rushed out of the gates to gather in the spoils. That day you could buy a loaf of bread in the city for a dime, and everyone ate their fill. Everyone, that is, except the captain of the guard. He was standing in the gate when the dinner bell rang and was trampled to death. Thus in one story we find illustrated both the miracle of movement and the danger of not moving: you could be trampled by those who are.

Finally, let me recall the parable about a football game between the big animals and the little animals. The big animals were winning by a wide margin, which is no surprise since football is a game in which big animals have a decided advantage. After the halftime break, the big animals took the field again. They sent the elephant up the middle. Surprise of surprises, he was tackled at the line of scrimmage. So they sent the rhinoceros around the right end, and he was tackled at the line of scrimmage. Finally they sent the hippopotamus around the left end, and he was tackled at the line of scrimmage. For the first time in the game the big animals had to punt, and the little animals had the ball. The quarterback, a squirrel, said in the huddle, "Before I call the first play, I want to know who was able to tackle the elephant coming up the middle." The centipede raised a hand and said, "I got the elephant." Then the quarterback asked, "Who got the rhinoceros coming around the right end?" The centipede said, "I got the rhino." So the squirrel asked, "Well, who was it that tackled the hippopotamus coming around the other end?" And again the centipede raised a hand. "Well," said the squirrel, "all I want to know is where were you during the first half?" The centipede replied, "I was tying my shoes."

There is a moral to this story: There is a time for preparation and a time to get in the game. All of these suggestions I have offered are no more than words on a bunch of pages unless you decide to put the ball in play. Life has never been a spectator sport. It's time for you to get into the game! And a wonderous game it is when engaged in by a fully alive, healthy, beautiful spirit.